STRAIGHT TALK
ABOUT
ALCOHOLISM

STRAIGHT TALK ABOUT ALCOHOLISM

ROBERT A. LIEBELT, Ph.D., M.D.
Introduction by Abraham J. Twerski, M.D.

PHAROS BOOKS
A SCRIPPS HOWARD COMPANY
NEW YORK

First published by Pharos Books in 1992.

Library of Congress Cataloging-in-Publication Data

Liebelt, Robert A.
Straight talk about alcoholism / Robert A. Liebelt :
introduction by Abraham J. Twerski.
        p.   cm.
Includes bibliographical references.
ISBN 0-88687-681-8
1. Alcoholism—Popular works.   2. Patient education.
I. Title.
RC565.L526   1992
616.86'1—dc20   91-43557   CIP

Pharos Books are available at special discounts on
bulk purchases for sales promotions, premiums,
fundraising or educational use. For details,
contact the Special Sales Department, Pharos
Books, 200 Park Avenue, New York, NY 10166.

Printed in the United States

Pharos Books
A Scripps Howard Company
200 Park Avenue
New York, New York 10166

10 9 8 7 6 5 4 3 2 1

FOREWORD

Each Tuesday afternoon for the past ten years, I have met with the patients of the Ignatia Hall Acute Alcohol and Drug Treatment Center at St. Thomas Medical Center in Akron. Sometimes it takes a little diplomatic and professional persuasion from the nursing staff to encourage some of the patients, especially those going through the early stages of alcohol withdrawal, to come and hear "another talk." Sometimes medical students, nursing students, and family members join us, and often we have visitors from Alcoholics Anonymous.

Beginning to speak as I printed "Alcoholism is a Disease, Or Crossing the Line" on the chalkboard, I told them I would describe how they got to be patients in Ignatia Hall. This usually caught their attention. As the doctor responsible for doing a complete medical history and physical examination at the time of admission, I already knew a great deal about each patient's medical and personal problems. I could make sure to highlight certain topics. Sometimes, if a patient nodded off momentarily, a fellow patient would nudge him awake, saying: "This is important for you to hear!" I saw that kind of caring peer pressure operating in the unit at all times.

Usually we would run well over the scheduled hour as we got carried away with questions and answers. Our record was two hours and twenty minutes. I mention this because I've been constantly amazed at the level of attention and interest the talk generated. I've lectured to medical, nursing, and dental students and just about every kind of health care professional for the past twenty-five years. None of these groups has been quite as attentive and eager to learn about a disease as this roomful of recovering alcoholics. They wanted to get all the help they could. It was the exception rather than the rule for a patient not to make a serious commitment to "work the program."

However, I found myself repeatedly embarrassed when one or more of the patients inevitably asked me if I had my talk written down so they could read and study it. Unfortunately, I have never lectured from notes, so I had nothing to offer—not even an outline. Occasionally I would say I was planning to write a book about the subject. Although the desire to write was there, I was always off doing something else—seeing patients, teaching a course in embryology to medical students, carrying out some research studies on nutrition and alcoholism, attending meetings, writing reports, and squeezing out all-too-little precious time for loved ones.

Then, one Tuesday afternoon, it happened. One of the patients, an engineer, raised his hand in a strikingly formal manner after the talk and, in a very sincere and almost pleading tone of voice, asked the usual question: "Do you have something written down so I can go over it again?" I gave him my then almost stock answer about writing a book. But he persisted, asking if I would just scribble down an outline or a handout. I was noncommittal. Then he said, "If only my five sons could read what you have just talked about, then maybe they would better understand what alcoholism is all about and take heed so they don't end up like their father!" I felt that if spending the time and effort in writing would help only one person, then it was worth it. That is how *Straight Talk About Alcoholism* had its beginning.

ACKNOWLEDGMENTS

To the many people who contributed indirectly to the writing of this book over the years, including relatives, friends, former teachers, pastors, and priests, as well as to many colleagues on the faculties of several medical schools, I say, "Many thanks!" I feel you know who you are. There are those who had a more direct influence on this book, and to you a very sincere, but simple, "Thank you!" Especially:

To my wonderful wife, Milotka, for her most perfectly timed "strokes" of encouragement, for asking the tough questions that had to be asked as she read each new draft, and for her help in working out the answers together.

To my mother, Helen, and my late father and grandfather, Arthur and Herman, for teaching me early in life to look always for the bright side of life and for the good side of every person.

To Ralph, Laurie, Erica, Nancy, and Kate for putting real meaning into the phrase "a proud father."

To Charlie Murdock for his persistence and encouragement when I was prepared to abandon this project.

To the staff of Ignatia Hall and the Interim Care Center, who have to be the most competent and caring people I will ever have the privilege to know.

To Dr. Ed Truitt, Jr., scientist, teacher, and colleague, for his phenomenal "memory bank" of scientific literature, which never failed to provide an answer to a question that arose while writing this book.

To Ed Truitt, III, writer, journalist, editor, and publisher, for his creative ideas, ability to grasp the essence of an idea, his feeling for words, and his willingness to make important decisions in a constructive manner, who made this writing venture a lot of fun and pleasure.

To the administration of St. Thomas Hospital and the medical staff for the opportunity to enter the alcoholism treatment field after an extended career in academic medicine, especially to Elaine Lee, Sandra Martin, and Lynda Grimm for dealing with many important details in the final stages of this book.

To Prudence Kohl for her encouragement and wisdom in guiding the process to its final accceptance.

To Hana Umlauf Lane, editor at Pharos Books, and her associates, for their most constructive suggestions and creative thoughts in bringing the message of this book to the reader who can benefit most.

To Dr. Abraham Twerski, M.D., who, without knowing it, introduced me to the problem of alcoholism many, many years ago during one of his outstanding talks in Youngstown, Ohio.

Finally, to all my patients for providing an almost daily inspiration by their courageous struggle with their disease during their hospital stay, and for returning to visit, even ten years later, with a proud smile on their faces to let us know "I'm doing great!" This is the moment in medicine that makes it all worthwhile.

Again, to all of you, "Many thanks!"

CONTENTS

INTRODUCTION

By Abraham J. Twerski, M.D.

While alcoholism has received much attention in the past two decades from health science professionals, industries, criminal justice systems, and public safety officials, there are valid reasons for even greater efforts to provide reliable and helpful data on the recognition and management of this disease.

Public education on the destructive effects of heroin and cocaine—AIDS, hepatitis, sudden death, psychosis, and crime— has been effective in discouraging some young people from using these drugs. Unfortunately, the desire for change of consciousness via chemicals has not diminished correspondingly, so that many studies which show a *decrease* in drug use among the young population show a concomitant *increase* in alcohol use. In other words, alcohol may be replacing heroin and cocaine, particularly among young people.

Second, the many advances of medical science have prolonged the average life span, so that the number of elderly people in the population is progressively increasing. Among this growing segment of the population are many persons who have retired, who are widowed, and whose socialization is limited by the death of friends or being housebound due to the wear-and-tear diseases of later life. An increasing number of elderly people, therefore, are seeking escape from the boredom of their existence, not via heroin or cocaine, but via alcohol.

Third, although much progress has been made in overcoming the attitudes of the Temperance and Prohibition era, there is a resurgence of opinion that considers alcoholism a sin or a moral weakness rather than a disease. This attitude may lead to a decrease in allotment of treatment resources and in recourse to ineffective methods of control of alcohol consumption.

The time is ripe, therefore, for a book that discusses and explains alcoholism from an authoritative medical viewpoint, describing the natural course of the disease, its varied symptoms, its treatment, and what is known about its causation, in a manner that is comprehensible to all, unencumbered by the professional jargon that so often obscures rather than enlightens. Dr. Liebelt has succeeded admirably in presenting complex data in a readily digestible form.

Straight Talk About Alcoholism should be read by everyone who has reason to learn more about alcoholism—physicians, psychotherapists, lawyers, employers, legislators, public officials, social agency workers, law enforcers, parents—by anyone who may be affected by alcoholism, either personally or in the family, and by anyone who should know what to look for in recognizing the disease in oneself or others, and what one should do and should not do. In short, *Straight Talk About Alcoholism* is a book that should really be read by everyone.

In Dr. Liebelt's presentation of the data and case histories, one can discern the consideration and empathy of a person sensitive to human suffering, but also one who would not hesitate to apply the firmness and assertiveness requisite for the effective treatment of serious and resistive disease. Thus, while Dr. Liebelt has made a conscious effort to tell us much about alcoholism, he has unknowingly also told us much about himself. As a result, we are the beneficiaries of two important items of knowledge.

AUTHOR'S INTRODUCTION

It is now more than fifty years since Ignatia Hall, one of the first medical treatment centers for alcoholism in this country, and, indeed, the world, was founded. Yet some half a century later, I find our society is still struggling with the questions "Is alcoholism really a disease?" and "Why do an estimated 100 million people drink in this country and about 10 million of them end up as alcoholics?" We're still a long way from knowing the answers to those questions. While there are countless books about the social, psychological, and behavioral aspects of alcoholism, I have found very few books written for the general public about the medical aspects of this widespread disease.

Since I am a physician who has been responsible for interviewing, examining, and studying the records of more than 5,000 Ignatia Hall patients over the past ten years, I want to share my firsthand impressions on the nature and progress of the disease of alcoholism. Most of what you read will be based on what I have heard with my own ears, seen with my own eyes, and felt with my own hands in this historic acute-care alcoholic treatment center.

Ignatia Hall's patient population is a cross section of the different socioeconomic groups of our community, from the indigent or nonpaying to executives of large corporations. About 80 percent of those who voluntarily admit themselves to the Ignatia Hall Acute Alcohol and Drug Treatment Center experience symptoms of physical dependency and go through the phase of withdrawal. Yet despite these dramatic symptoms of a disease at work, the stereotype of the alcoholic remains "the drunken bum in the gutter" image. I emphasize that alcoholism has no socioeconomic barriers. The behavior and actions of a drunken person are an expression of the alcohol acting on his or her brain and body.

When the effects of the alcohol gradually subside with abstinence over a three-to-five-day period, in most instances you will find a very caring, sensitive, and loving person. I can speak with some authority on this point, because it is true for the majority of my patients when they leave our unit to return home. The challenge when they are discharged, of course, is to prevent that real person from once again being disguised by alcohol.

Half a century ago, Dr. Bob, co-founder of Alcoholics Anonymous, was sneaking alcoholics up the back stairs of Akron area hospitals in order to help them through the dangerous detoxification phase of recovery. The medical world of the time was not ready to treat alcoholism like any other disease. Finally, Dr. Bob approached Sister Ignatia, registrar of St. Thomas Hospital in Akron, to see if she would admit his patients. Her basic question was "Are these patients sick?" Dr. Bob convinced her that the answer was

"Yes," and thus St. Thomas Hospital became one of the first hospitals in the world to establish an alcoholic ward.

However, because of its long history and complex social and behavioral dimensions, alcoholism is a slippery disease to diagnose and treat. We'll attempt to answer the difficult questions such as "Who is an alcoholic?" and "Why do people drink?"

There are laboratory tests like measuring blood sugar (glucose level) to diagnose diabetes, or taking a chest X-ray to diagnose pneumonia, or an electrocardiogram to detect heart disease, but no reliable test to detect alcoholism in its early stages. We'll discuss the strengths and weaknesses of the various questionnaires to determine a person's drinking pattern.

Clinicians have been able to draw clear lines between the stages of the disease process of diabetes mellitus so that we can say who is and who isn't a diabetic. We'll compare diabetes to alcoholism to make a working model of the disease and draw some lines to suggest who is and who isn't an alcoholic.

I compare alcoholism to my own genetically determined disease—lactose intolerance—and describe how I deal with it by avoiding milk products. I can describe alcoholism in the same context as a *genetically determined disease* that is *progressive* and *terminal*. The "don't drink" approach makes the same medical sense for the alcoholic as avoiding milk products does for my lactose intolerance.

From these perspectives, I'll give a working definition of alcoholism. That is, we can view alcoholism as *an incurable disease* that begins (officially) at the time of diagnosis and ends at the time of death. No one can cure this disease, just as we cannot cure diabetes mellitus, but we can manage or control it during the "interim period" by a lifelong treatment program that can result in a happy, normal, and productive life span. At present, the treatment for alcoholism is education and persuasion plus coercion to enter a treatment program.

From reviewing the more than 5,000 detailed medical and psychosocial histories of our patients over the past ten years, I find that over 80 percent have already "crossed the line" into physical dependency by the time they are admitted. We have compiled many warning signs revealed in the medical and social histories of those who have crossed the line. These include: experiencing blackouts, DWI (Driving While Intoxicated) tickets, warnings on the job about drinking, experiencing palpitations of the heart, and frequent diarrhea, to list a few.

Despite this alarming list of signs and symptoms, there is a tremendous problem convincing anyone that he or she does indeed have a drinking problem. This is called "denial." I'll give examples of various forms, such as stuporous, stupid, and secretive denial. We'll talk about the technique of intervention used in breaking through this denial and getting someone to voluntarily enter a much needed treatment program. Our list proves valuable to the 15 to 20 percent of our patients who are not certain whether they do or do not have a problem.

Our warning signs also include genetic factors. For instance, our study reveals that over half of our male patients and a similar percentage of our female patients report that they have (or had, before his death) a father who is alcoholic. The recent "adoption studies" in Europe shed even more light on the genetic connection, as do the studies we are carrying out on experimental animals. We will touch on how genetic factors influence changes in brain chemistry. Like any drug, alcohol has very important pharmacological actions that need to be considered. Alcohol acts as an anesthetic agent no matter what age or state of the disease process. The levels of anesthesia which we talk about in more detail are: (1) euphoria, (2) amnesia (blackouts), (3) relaxation, and (4) death. The message is that when an individual consumes "a significant amount" of alcohol, he is essentially anesthetizing himself as part of becoming drunk.

I've dedicated a special section to the matter of alcoholism and women. It has been suggested that as women leave the privacy of their homes to join the work force and become more visible, we will see an increased prevalence of alcoholism in women; it will no longer be seen as a "man's disease." Comparing the records of male and female patients in our treatment center suggests that the disease is the same in women and in men, just as diabetes is the same disease in both sexes, with the usual individual variations. The major differences found so far can be related to the "double standard" of sexism in our society, which creates added burdens for the recovering female alcoholic.

As in my weekly "chalk talks" to my patients, I will spend some time detailing the various physical and chemical effects of alcohol on the body and describing the progress through the various stages of alcoholism. Most of my patients ask, "How's my liver, Doc?" They are usually relieved to hear that the liver has the ability to heal itself after alcohol is withdrawn.

"Some Thoughts About the Future" focuses on where we

are going as scientists in our attempt to unravel the complexities of this disease. There is a need for changes in public attitudes in light of recent research, particularly the superiority of "I can handle it, why can't you?" The new findings indicate over and over again that alcoholism is an inherited disease. We need to define and detail the disease in biological terms, so that one day it may be possible, during infancy or early childhood, to predict who will and who will not be susceptible to developing the disease. If we could accomplish this, perhaps we could use appropriate education and guidance for preventing the damage caused by alcoholism.

One of the significant breakthroughs of our times has been our increased understanding of how diet alters and influences the chemistry of the brain. Studies have shown that introducing naturally occurring chemicals—amino acids—to our diet can help alleviate depression and sleeplessness. This undoubtedly will lead to the design of more specific pharmacological agents that will act on specific parts of our brains, especially the "happy" or "pleasure" center(s).

The role of biofeedback techniques in modifying behavior—like learning to cope with stress—is attracting attention as we learn more each day to convince us that "thinking about it" can influence certain body functions like heart rate and blood pressure.

All of these exciting findings give cause for optimism, but our enthusiasm must be tempered by watchful waiting to avoid false hopes and expectations. The pathways of research can be very long, with many curves.

Finally, I have made no attempt to footnote all the references to support each of the thoughts, ideas, and concepts of this book. I did not intend to write a scholarly work for professionals, or the "last word" on current research. Rather, I want to provide a readable and understandable guide to the medical aspects of alcoholism for my patients, their families, friends, fellow workers, and neighbors. However, I have included a list of further reading for those interested in gaining more information about certain topics covered in the book.

I could not have written this without the excellent support and efforts of Ignatia Hall's "health team"—the doctors, nurses, aides, counselors, social workers, secretary, and even the housekeeping staff. I have constantly appreciated and respected the staff's spirit of camaraderie and caring, and have seen that spirit taken up by the patients.

Just a word or two to my patients: "Many thanks for all you have taught me. I consider it an honor and a privilege that I can count each of you among my friends!" And, as a guiding principle that Dr. Bob often reminded Mr. Bill W. of when they were developing the guidelines for Alcoholics Anonymous, I have tried to "keep it simple."

ONE

From "Devil" to Disease: A Brief History

Alcoholism is not a new disease. Historically, I think we can safely assume that if alcohol was available, the disease was probably present. Paintings on the walls of caves show people brewing beer, which suggests the presence of drinking behavior in mankind from the beginnings of human history.

There are more than seventy-five passages about drunkenness in the Bible, and many of them depict alcoholism and alcoholic behaviors if we translate them into modern terms and definitions. The second thing Noah did on disembarking from the ark was to plant a vineyard (first he built an altar). And the next thing we know, Noah was passed out drunk! (Gen. 9:20–26). For a perfect description of an alcohol-induced blackout, read about the deception of Lot by his daughters (Gen. 19:30–35). From cave paintings to some of our earliest religious and historical writings, drinking, drunkenness, and a chronic, progressive disease known as alcoholism have been part of the human condition.

Yet it wasn't until the mid-1800s—less than 150 years ago—that the studies of Louis Pasteur revealed the existence of living creatures unseen by the unaided eye, called bacteria, that were responsible for causing certain kinds of infectious diseases. Prior to his work, contagious diseases were thought to be caused by some mysterious power or by the vapors from swamps. Pasteur's studies also revealed that these microscopic creatures were capable of fermenting or converting sugar solutions to a chemical—CH_3CH_2OH, or ethyl alcohol (ethanol)—the key ingredient of every alcoholic beverage, whether beer, wine, whiskey, gin, vodka, or what have you. For the first time, people began to realize that the effect of this chemical in alcoholic beverages was the root of the disease of alcoholism.

Early 1900s—The U.S. Temperance Movement

Following the Civil War, and into the early 1900s, the impact of alcohol on our society was becoming more pronounced and visible. There were more crimes, suicides, homicides, disturbances of the peace, and family disruptions linked to alcohol and drinking. Or, at least the drinking was being publicly acknowledged as either a cause or a factor in social upheaval.

The anti-drinking movement that developed in this country focused mostly upon "the drunkard" and "his poor family." From church pulpits throughout the land came hellfire-and-brimstone sermons condemning "Demon Rum," "the Evils of Drinking," and "the Work of the Devil." The attitude was that drinking was a moral problem, and a drunkard was viewed as immoral—a sinner who, because of weakness in his or her character, needed to be "saved."

This attitude remains embedded in our society and its laws today. For instance, two ex-servicemen afflicted with the disease of alcoholism claimed they were unable to take advantage of their Veterans' Administration educational benefits during their eligible time period because they were disabled by the disease. They argued that Veterans' Administration policy recognized physical and mental disability as justification for extension. Alcoholism certainly qualifies on both grounds. However, the Veterans' Administration denied their appeal based on a VA policy adopted in the 1930s that viewed alcoholism as an act of "willful misconduct." The U.S. Supreme Court, in April 1988, ruled in favor of the Veterans' Administration.

Certainly there is a "willful" and behavioral component to alcoholism, but the point of this book is to examine its physiological roots and the natural history of the disease.

Only in the last fifty years have we begun to see alcoholism more clearly as a very specific disease. As such, moralistic finger-pointing and arguments about will and willpower seem irrelevant, if not outright harmful to recovery and treatment.

In the early 1900s, certain women decided upon an approach more direct than thundering from the pulpit. They chose drastic action against what they saw as the source of the problem—alcoholic beverages. Under the leadership of Carrie Nation, the Women's Christian Temperance Union dedicated itself to the elimination of drinking. The WCTU's practical solution to the problem was to smash the kegs and bottles in saloons, taverns, and bars. Armed with axes and clubs, these women would assault local drinking establishments and leave them in shambles. On the surface, it seemed a reasonable idea, but it didn't work. They were up against a millennia-old disease process, not a finite amount of ethyl alcohol. People continued to drink.

1919–1932—The Prohibition Era

With the failure of temperance efforts on the local level, the next move was to address the problem on a national level and enlist the force and authority of the U.S. government. In 1919 Congress passed the Volstead Act, better known as Prohibition. The law virtually prohibited the sale and consumption of alcoholic beverages in the United States. After thirteen years of increased crime, corruption, bootlegging, moonshining, speak-easies, bathtub gin, and home brew, Franklin D. Roosevelt signed the repeal of the act in 1932 in one of his first acts as president.

Although statistics showed some decrease in alcohol consumption during Prohibition, viewed in retrospect, this law was doomed to failure from the outset. Unlike many diseases, especially those caused by bacteria or viruses that can be controlled by public health laws—testing drinking waters, vaccinations, and quarantines—some diseases cannot be legislated away. Carried to the extreme, it would be like passing a law that requires anyone with the disease of diabetes to eat only the prescribed number of calories in his meals and inject the prescribed number of units of insulin. This approach doesn't work because of the individuality of the disease process. More about this analogy later.

1935—Founding of Alcoholics Anonymous (AA)

In 1935 a very significant event occurred in Akron, Ohio, that forever changed the way alcoholism is treated. The outcome of this chance meeting continues to be the most effective means of treating alcoholism to the present day. An Akron physician (Dr. Bob) and a New York businessman (Bill W.) had what many have come to feel was a predestined meeting in the Mayflower Hotel in downtown Akron. Both of these men were afflicted with the disease of alcoholism. With the help of tire heiress Henrietta Seiberling, and the assistance of several clergy and members of the Oxford Group, a religious spiritual fellowship, the guiding principles of Alcoholics Anonymous were formulated.

The foundation of the AA program is the concept that one must treat the body, the mind, and the soul, and that all three of these aspects of the individual must be involved if there is to be any semblance of success. Actually, this approach is now widely accepted in the treatment of all diseases and is labeled wholistic medicine. Some prefer to spell it "holistic" to make certain we do not forget the role of the holy, or the spiritual dimension in the healing process.

1939—Ignatia Hall at St. Thomas Medical Center

In 1939 another significant milestone in the treatment of alcoholism took place in Akron. What is probably the nation's first medical unit dedicated to the treatment of alcoholism was formed. Since then thousands have been treated in the Ignatia Hall Acute Alcohol Treatment Center.

Dr. Bob had been taking his alcoholic patients to another

Akron hospital. The story has it that he would have to sneak a patient up the back stairs of the hospital and persuade the nurses to let him use an empty room. The moral and legal issues of drunkenness were still very much to the fore. Dr. Bob would then sit with the patient for three or four days, feeding him or her Karo syrup, tomato juice, and sauerkraut—a seemingly unlikely combination of foods for a sick person. Yet, as one analyzed what was going on in the patient's body, one saw there were some very good medical reasons for this treatment for withdrawal from alcohol, or "detox" as it is commonly called. We know, for example, that sugar in the diet, especially fruit sugars (fructose), will speed up the metabolism or clearance of alcohol from the blood. (The idea that black coffee will sober up an intoxicated person is a myth. The caffeine in the coffee will only produce a "wide-awake drunk." Otherwise, you will have a sleepy drunk to deal with.) Today we encourage our patients to drink as much orange or other fruit juices as they can handle when first admitted to the center.

The tomato juice was equally important, because alcohol is a potent dehydrating agent. That's why you wake up "the morning after" with a cottony, sticky, dry mouth. The mucus in the saliva is 99 percent water, and when the water is removed it leaves behind the sticky mucus component of saliva from the salivary glands, which have also been shut down by the alcohol. Water makes up about 70 percent of our body weight—a person who weighs 100 pounds is carrying around 70 pounds of water—and can be reduced by alcohol acting on centers in the brain. This, in turn, can cause changes in salt or electrolyte content of the body. Disturbances in the salt content are believed to be partially responsible for the excruciating muscle cramps or "charley horses" experienced by many people who are drinking large quantities of alcohol. Dr. Bob's tomato juice served two purposes: (1) to rehydrate the patient without using intravenous fluids, and (2) more importantly perhaps, because it is so rich in sodium, potassium, chloride, and salts, to start bringing the electrolyte components back to normal.

Finally, sauerkraut is a rich source of vitamin B_1. This vitamin can be depleted to a deficiency state within seven to ten days after you stop eating. I often hear "When I drink, I don't eat" from patients newly admitted to the center. The effects of vitamin B_1 deficiency will be discussed more fully later, but for now let me explain that we assume each patient entering treatment to be poorly nourished, and they are injected daily with 100mg of thiamine (vitamin B_1) for four days after admission. Firsthand observation has shown us that the strange combination therapy used by Dr. Bob was not just something grabbed out of the air. It was, in fact, a rational treatment for the problem, given the resources available in the 1930s.

By 1939 Dr. Bob began to encounter some resistance to his first treatment program, not because it wasn't proving to be successful, but rather because of the attitudes of the hospital administration and his fellow physicians. The message to him was that all these drunks he was bringing to the hospital were giving it a bad name. (How far we've come since 1939!) In any event, Dr. Bob was asked to take his drunken patients elsewhere, but there appeared to be nowhere else to go in Akron. Finally, he tried St. Thomas Hospital "up on the hill." Sister Ignatia was the registrar at the time, responsible for deciding who would be admitted to the hospital. The story goes that when Dr. Bob approached Sister Ignatia, she asked him only one question: "Are these patients sick?"

Dr. Bob had no problem answering "Yes!"

"Then certainly we will admit them," she said, "and they will come in the front door like all the other patients."

Thus, St. Thomas Hospital became one of the first to open its doors for the medical treatment of alcoholism. Furthermore, the formation of St. Thomas's alcoholic ward in 1939 represented the first real recognition of alcoholism as a specific medical problem or disease.

The 1950s—The Disease Concept

In the 1950s, the American Medical Association first published a report which stated that alcoholism is a *chronic* disease, it is *progressive*, with occurrence of *relapses*, and, if untreated, will lead to medical *complications* and, indeed, *death*. Despite the tremendous significance of this report, it apparently fell upon closed eyes and deaf ears within the medical profession, because even today many physicians are very limited in their understanding of the disease of alcoholism. This landmark report makes several very important points.

A Chronic Disease

First, a *chronic disease* is one which may take months or years to develop before it can be detected. You do not become an alcoholic overnight. For example, in taking a detailed medical history of each patient during admission, I always ask, "When was the first time you ever *tasted alcohol*?" There is a wide range of answers. More than one patient has told me he was six months old at the time. When I challenged them, saying they couldn't even hold a glass in their hands at six months, the reply was "My mother told me she would stick her finger in a shot glass full of whiskey and rub it on my gums when I was teething!" I had to agree that this was the first time the patient had tasted alcohol, and I've come to realize this is still a widespread practice that takes advantage of the anesthetizing effects of alcohol. However, among more than 5,000 patients, the average age for the first taste of alcohol is twelve years for the males and fifteen for the females.

Then I ask, "How old were you when you first recognized you had a problem with alcohol, or do you have a problem?" Interestingly, approximately 20 percent of our patients will either deny or question whether they have a drinking problem (more about the problem of denial later). The remaining 80 percent readily state "I have a problem with alcohol." The average age of all these patients (male and female) when they first sought treatment at Ignatia Hall is thirty-five years, suggesting that it takes approximately twenty years for the disease to develop to the point where people are seeking treatment. This is consistent with the characteristics of any chronic disease. However, I should emphasize that this is an average age. The actual age for patients admitted to our center ranges from eighteen to eighty-nine years, which means there are tremendous individual differences as to the time of onset of the disease and how fast it progresses, as well as when help is sought.

It should not be surprising to find individuals at the two extremes of the age span. Recently, during a presentation to high school students, I met a student who had entered a treatment program for alcoholism while in the seventh grade! On the other hand, one of the oldest patients ever admitted to Ignatia Hall was an eighty-eight-year-old woman who, up to the age of seventy-five, drank one or two glasses of wine *a week* when she and her husband went out to dinner. Then her husband died. She became lonely and depressed. And within a period of five to seven years, she developed a very serious alcohol problem, including severe liver damage. As she remarked when admitted to our center, "Doc, all I have are my dogs and my beer."

A Progressive Disease

The *progressiveness* of the disease is more difficult to pin down. Old-timers in AA always remark that "It is never going to get better, it always gets worse." When I entered this field, I heard stories about how an alcoholic who had achieved sobriety would, if he started drinking again, soon reach the point where he would have been had he been drinking all along.

Initially, I was skeptical of this type of report, but now I am convinced that it actually happens in certain patients. Within just a few days of drinking again, they find themselves very sick in both mind and body. Years before, it would have taken weeks or months of steady drinking for them to reach a comparable point.

Part of this response could be explained by the development of tolerance over the years of drinking and the loss of this tolerance with sobriety. Referring to Figure 1, at Point A, the individual may have had a drinking pattern of "one or two beers a day" or less. At Point B, a daily intake of up to a case of beer or a quart of whiskey was tolerated. Then, at

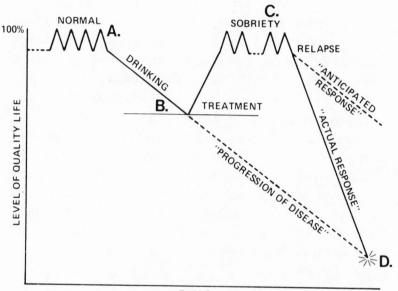

FIGURE 1—A depiction of the progression of the disease of alcoholism. Point A represents a drinking pattern of "one to two beers a day" or less. At Point B the alcoholic can tolerate a case of beer or a quart of whiskey a day. By Point C, the person's tolerance has returned to the level of Point A. Point D is reached more rapidly with each relapse.

Point C, the individual's tolerance has returned to that of Point A, or even lower. At this time, even though the mind may think a case of beer or a quart of whiskey can be handled as it was before, the body responds to "the first drink" with dramatic effects. Soon the individual is right back at Point B and then progresses rapidly to Point D.

However, tolerance is not the complete answer. Recently, scientists studying the effects of certain drugs on the brains of animals have observed what some consider a similar type of event. A convulsion or seizure can be induced in an animal with a certain dose of a drug. Then, after the animal has recovered and returned to an apparently normal state, a smaller dose of the same drug will produce the same seizure effect. Scientists have called this the "kindling effect"—using smaller pieces of wood to start large logs burning.

There are also other events taking place in the body during the time it takes to reach Point D. For want of a better term, let us call it simply an aging process. As we get older, our bodily functions change, especially in how we handle drugs and medications. Physicians dealing with elderly patients have long learned to adjust the dose of a drug according to a person's age. This brings us back to the maxim "It never gets better, it always gets worse" each time one "falls off the wagon."

Relapse

Starting to drink again after a period of sobriety is called a *relapse*. I have seen a patient discharged at 9:00 A.M., leave the hospital, head down the street to a bar, and begin drinking again by 9:30 A.M. (Sometimes they run down the street, and the starting time is 9:20.) On the other hand, we have seen patients relapse who had been sober for as long as 22 years.

Medical Complications

The *complications* from alcohol in terms of medical problems can involve almost every organ in the body. The only organ that seems to be spared, for some unknown reason, is the kidney. All the others—the brain, eyes, lungs, heart, stomach, large intestine, pancreas, testes, ovaries, skin, muscles, bone marrow, immune system—are affected by alcohol. Everyone seems to be aware of the vulnerability of the liver, and there is good reason to be concerned about the liver when consuming large quantities of alcohol.

There are two points I would like to emphasize. The first is that of all the alcohol you put into your mouth, almost none of it comes out the other end. Ninety-five percent of the alcohol you drink is absorbed into the circulation. The second point is that all the veins that drain the stomach and intestine come together and empty the blood into the liver before it enters the systemic circulation through the heart. An in-house saying at St. Thomas is that if you drink a bottle of whiskey, it is like pouring that bottle of whiskey over your liver. The liver metabolizes about 90 percent of the alcohol absorbed into the body—that is, converts it into other substances. About 5 percent is exhaled through the lungs, permitting the use of a breath analyzer to measure blood alcohol concentration. The remaining 5 percent is excreted in the urine.

The liver metabolizes, or breaks down, alcohol into carbon dioxide, water, and energy as follows:

$$CH_3CH_2OH \rightarrow \text{Metabolism or}$$
$$\text{breakdown} \rightarrow CO_2 + H_2O + \text{Energy}$$

A few remarks about the caloric content of alcoholic beverages: A shot glass of whiskey has about 150 calories, a glass of wine (3–4 oz.) about 100 calories, and a bottle of beer (excluding the light brands) about 250 to 300 calories. People do not realize how many calories they are taking in when they consume large quantities of alcoholic beverages. Several years ago, a sportscaster noted that the athletes in the Olympic Games ate and drank as much as 4,000 calories a day. Considering that the average adult consumes about 2,000 calories a day, this is obviously a significant increase that goes along with the rigors of training and competing. But a simple calculation reveals that many of our patients who report that they drank a case of beer daily were consuming 6,000 to 7,000 calories a day (24 beers times 250 to 300 calories per bottle). One patient reported that he was drinking at least a gallon of fortified wine (minimum 20 percent alcohol content) in addition to an occasional meal; rough calculations put his daily caloric intake at about 8,500 calories. Many of our patients remark that they can't understand why they are gaining weight when they don't eat anything. It is indeed a sobering experience for them when we calculate the caloric intake for each day they were drinking.

Yet in spite of these striking caloric intakes almost daily, some patients continue to maintain body leanness while others develop the so-called classic beer belly. To analyze this seeming discrepancy, we have been carrying out various types of body measurements, including skin-fold thickness determinations (anthropometric analyses). Preliminary findings suggest the genetic factors, rather than caloric intake, whether it comes from food or alcoholic beverages, determine whether the patient maintains a body leanness or becomes obese.

Although alcoholic beverages provide energy, they have

no nutritional value. They are devoid of adequate nutrients necessary for good nutritional support of bodily functions. The situation that develops is similar to the problem I frequently encounter with my car. I usually use the self-service gas pumps when filling my car with gasoline. After the fill-up, I drive off and return when the fuel gauge again shows the tank is close to empty. Again I fill it up, pay the attendant, and drive off. Unfortunately, I don't take the time to check the air pressure on the tires, the engine oil, windshield wiper fluid, and brake or transmission fluid. Then came the day when the engine stalled at every stop light. Finally, the mechanic discovered that the air cleaner was filthy—so clogged with dirt the engine could barely get air. As soon as it was replaced, the car drove normally.

This is like what happens to a person who is getting most of his energy from alcohol. He goes to work every day, goes to church on Sunday, does chores around the house, and seems to be living a normal life. But eventually the lack of proper nutrients like vitamins, minerals, trace elements, and proteins that are essential for healthy functioning of the body's machinery will cause it to break down. This might be the first time medical assistance is sought.

It is amazing to see the reaction of patients who realize what was missing after years of running on only seven cylinders instead of the eight their body can generate. "I never realized I could feel this good!" they often exclaim.

At St. Thomas we have come to assume that in addition to many other medical problems, and despite their body weight, our patients are also suffering from the effects of malnutrition, whether they know it or not. Our staff makes sure there is plenty of food on hand in the center, and part of our program is a series of discussions on good nutrition.

Parents regularly criticize young people for eating junk food: sugar-coated cereals, candy bars, and pop. Nothing could be more of a junk food than the adult alcoholic beverage. It is small wonder that 40 to 50 percent of our patients complain of numbness and tingling in their hands and feet—a symptom of severe deficiency in vitamin B_1 or thiamine, which can develop in as little as ten days with poor nutrition. More about thiamine later.

When alcohol is metabolized in the liver, the alcohol does not go directly to CO_2, H_2O, and energy in one step, but through a series of intermediate steps, which have their own effects:

$$CH_3CH_2OH \rightarrow CH_3\overset{\displaystyle O}{\overset{\displaystyle \|}{CH}} \rightarrow CH_3COOH \rightarrow$$
$$CO_2 + H_2O + Energy$$

The first breakdown product of alcohol is acetaldehyde: $CH_3CH=0$.

If we were to take a bottle of acetaldehyde from the chemist's laboratory and give some to anyone, within a short time—minutes, or even seconds—our unfortunate subject would experience: (1) a hot-flush sensation about the face and neck, (2) a cold, clammy sweat, (3) pounding and racing (palpitations) of the heart, (4) nausea with vomiting or the "dry heaves," (5) a headache with the sensation of intense pain just inches from the head, and (6) extreme irritability— "Don't let the cat walk across the room, I feel it all over!"

These symptoms, of course, are commonly ascribed to the severe hangover that follows drinking too much. Acetaldehyde, sometimes called the hangover chemical, is considered the cause of much of the misery associated with the aftereffects of drinking too much alcohol.

To emphasize the importance of the role of breakdown products of any chemical taken into the body, let me explain the detrimental effects of methanol (CH_3OH), sometimes called wood alcohol, when ingested. When I was growing up, I remember adults warning children "Never drink wood alcohol, it will make you go blind!" What happens when wood alcohol (CH_3OH) is taken into the body instead of "grain" alcohol (CH_3CH_2OH)? It also goes to the liver, where it is broken down into:

$$CH_3OH \rightarrow HCOH \rightarrow CO_2 + H_2O + Energy$$

In this case, instead of *acetaldehyde*, a compound called *formaldehyde* is formed—one of the main ingredients of embalming fluid. When a person drinks wood alcohol, they are, in effect, embalming themselves from the inside out. Even in small doses, formaldehyde taken internally can cause blindness, damage to other organs, and even death. It is a potent poison.

Acetaldehyde is not quite as toxic as formaldehyde, yet it is probably a main cause of cellular damage in many organs of the body. The expression "Every man makes his own poison" applies directly to the alcoholic patient. That's exactly what the liver does to alcohol; it converts it into a significantly more toxic substance—a poison whose amount varies with the volume of alcohol consumed.

The accumulation of high concentrations of acetaldehyde in the liver undoubtably plays a major role in liver damage by producing what is called, in the early stages, acute alcoholic hepatitis. This is a condition in which the liver becomes swollen and tender, causing pain to the right side of the belly just below the ribs. The first stage of the continual injury caused by acetaldehyde, or any similar toxin in the liver, is the accumulation of fat in the liver cells, a condition called a fatty liver. This will cause it to be large but not necessarily tender. Continued injury, however, will result in the destruction of numerous liver cells, and the resulting empty spaces are filled in with scar tissue, which is called cirrhosis. Advanced cirrhosis of the liver causes a swollen belly filled with fluid (ascites), yellow skin (jaundice), internal and external bleeding, and wasting of the body—in short, a terrible road to an inevitable and painful death.

Fortunately for many of our patients, one of the amazing properties of the liver is its ability to heal itself, or to regenerate. This was first suggested by a study done in 1931 by scientist George Higgins at the Mayo Clinic.

Dr. Higgins made a simple but dramatic experiment. He performed surgery on laboratory rats, exposed the liver, and cut away two-thirds of it. He left the remnant of the liver in place, sutured up the abdominal wall wound, and returned the animals to their cages. Four to six weeks later, he took the same animals, reopened the abdomens, and found that the livers had returned to their original size! The rat liver has an amazing capacity to regenerate new cells when injured. The same is true of the human liver and for many other species of animals as well. Unfortunately, the liver that has been replaced by scar tissue (cirrhosis) has lost this regenerative capacity.

Most of our patients come to us with only minimal or moderate damage to their livers. Using the level of certain enzymes and other chemicals in the blood as indicators, we can assess the degree of damage and the rate at which the liver heals or regenerates during the treatment program. The best treatment for alcohol-induced liver injury? Good diet, rest, no alcohol, and time. Describing similar complications that occur in all organs of the body is beyond the scope of this book, but detailed descriptions are to be found in any medical pathology textbook.

Death

The final characteristic of alcoholism referred to in the American Medical Association report was *death* in those cases that went untreated. The average age at which an alcoholic will die of medical complications if untreated is estimated to be in the fifth decade of life. The average age does not include deaths occurring at any age from suicide, homicide, or accidents. The youngest alcohol-induced death we have ever witnessed at our center was a twenty-six-year-old patient who had started drinking at fourteen years of age. By the time he came to us for his first treatment, his liver was essentially destroyed. He died sixty days after admission.

Aside from those five important characteristics, the significance of the American Medical Association report is the fact that all chronic diseases treated by medical science follow the same conceptual model: chronic, progressive, relapses, complications, and death. For example, diabetes mellitus is a chronic disease that shows up in many people at middle age. It is a progressive disease in that changes in diet and frequent doses of insulin are required over time to control blood sugar levels. Failure to comply with a specific diet and insulin schedule will cause the disease to worsen. Relapses occur in the sense that a patient in good control may go out of control during stressful situations, for a variety of reasons. Untreated, diabetes causes complications including damage to the blood vessels in the retina of the eye, resulting in blindness; to the kidneys; and to the smaller blood vessels supplying the feet and legs, which, in extreme circumstances, can lead to amputation. And, of course, untreated diabetes mellitus can lead to an earlier death.

We can use this same chronic-disease model to describe heart disease leading to congestive heart failure, to describe lung diseases such as emphysema, and even to predict the course of some cancers.

1960s to the Present—Evolution of the Medical Model

The medical approach to a disease is usually a two-pronged effort. On one hand, the clinician at the bedside is looking for signs and symptoms and attempting to develop an understanding of the course of the disease from early to late stages. He or she is examining firsthand the effect of the disease on the whole organism, the whole person, to understand the interaction of the various systems and organs in that complex whole. On the other hand, the scientist working in the laboratory or carrying out bench research is directing attention to the causes of the disease at the level of specific organs, cells, and even molecules. Bridging the two, a whole range of biomedical research is attempting to gain new understanding of how the chemical, cellular, and molecular processes work in the real world of disease and recovery.

Three major areas of biomedical research, both basic and clinical, have provided us with a much better understanding of the disease of alcoholism in the past forty years. These ground-breaking areas include:

1) *How the Cells of the Body Work*   Development of more and more powerful microscopes and centrifuges has permitted scientists to literally take the cell apart down to the level of molecules and atoms. These efforts have provided very convincing evidence that many diseases start at the molecular level of the cell.

This concept of the molecular basis for disease says that any disruption of the molecules of the cell can bring about repercussions at every level of physical organization, such as cells, tissues, organs, and body systems. As each new level is disrupted, different signs and symptoms appear, until the individual's physical and emotional changes will have an effect on the members of the family and on the community at large. The recent AIDS crisis amply demonstrates how the breakdown of immune responses at a cellular level can cause dramatic personal, social, legal, and economic changes in the world community.

Basic scientists are accumulating evidence that alcohol has specific effects on the molecules that make up the membranes of cells, especially of the brain cells. These changes in the cell membrane cause changes in the individual's physical and emotional state. Alcohol can also act upon other elements of the cell machinery, throwing a proverbial monkey wrench into the works. The cells become damaged to produce a swollen, painful liver, or a bleeding ulcer, or an irregularly beating heart, or damage to any other organ of the body.

2) *How the Brain Works* In spite of the overwhelming complexity of the human brain, by slow, deliberate, and painstaking efforts, researchers have begun to shed a glimmer of light on how this mysterious part of the body works. We know now, for example, that specific parts of the brain control certain body functions. A blow to the back of the head could injure the occipital lobe of the brain and cause sudden blindness. A ruptured blood vessel with bleeding (a stroke) in the side of the brain called the parietal lobe could result in the inability to talk or even walk, depending upon the amount and location of the bleeding. The region of the brain called the hypothalamus regulates our pituitary gland, which in turn regulates the flow of body hormones.

Recently, an area of the brain has been discovered that controls our sense of pleasure when we eat some wonderful food, drink some especially tasty beverage, or even engage in sexual pleasure. This area of the brain is called the primary reward center, or better still, the happy center. Stimulation of this area of the brain in laboratory animals can result in a behavior pattern of searching, craving, and a compulsiveness that does not go away unless the stimulation is stopped or the desire is fulfilled. These types of studies have led to the notion that all human and animal behavior is a reflection of changes in brain chemistry at the cellular and molecular levels.

What is most exciting is the accumulating evidence that even what we eat can affect our daily moods and behavior.

For example, the level of hyperactivity in a child can be reduced when sugar and other sweets are removed from the diet. Viewed from a cellular and nutritional standpoint, the craving for a drink and the loss of control when drinking leave little doubt there is fertile ground for this line of research in alcoholism. Indeed, research into nutrition on a cellular level has already added to our understanding of the disease of alcoholism.

3) How Inheritance and Genetics Work   The field of genetics has advanced dramatically since the first report from a monk tending his garden in a Swiss monastery in the 1800s. This monk, Gregor Mendel, took sweetpea plants with red flowers and sweetpea plants with white flowers and cross-pollinated them to produce seeds that grew into sweetpea plants with pink flowers. This provided the scientific basis for observations made for centuries that "He looks just like his father" or "Her red hair is just like her mother's." Today, using the basic principles observed in that monastery garden, geneticists have provided us with seedless watermelons, turkeys with breasts that double the amount of white meat, thoroughbred race horses, and many other innovations.

Developments in the field of human genetics have been just as dramatic. Specific diseases such as certain types of leukemia and Down's syndrome (still often miscalled Mongolian idiocy) are both genetically determined. A growing list of birth defects like harelip, cleft palate, club foot, heart defects, cataracts of the eyes, and different forms of mental retardation have all been traced to specific genetic roots. As technological advances provide us with instruments to study more closely how the body cells work, scientists are uncovering genetically controlled disturbances in the chemistry of certain cells that cause diseases like diabetes and different kinds of cancer, hardening of the arteries, and various types of mental illness.

Alcoholism was more or less accepted for years as running in families. But this idea created much confusion and controversy—how much was due to being raised in a drinking environment (there was always wine on the table) and how much was due to inheritance or genetics, i.e., the differences between your cells and my cells unless we are identical twins. Only in the past few years have scientists uncovered evidence showing the genetic basis for developing the disease of alcoholism, whether raised in a drinking or nondrinking environment. I refer to the various twin studies revealing that when identical twins born to alcoholic parents were put up for adoption before three years of age, whether they grew up in a foster home in which drinking took place or one where it did not, both would grow up to be alcoholics. The classic nature vs. nurture argument was resoundingly tipped in favor of nature, with the genes and cells themselves being the most fundamental determining factor in the development of alcoholism.

These genetic studies are now being carried out at the molecular level to show how the rate and chemical pathway of metabolism taken by alcohol in the body may vary greatly from one person to another. Scientists are particularly interested in studying these differences because, for one thing, a distinct difference in basic metabolism could be used to possibly *predict* who is most likely to become an alcoholic and who is not long before the disease develops. Remember our average time of onset and progression. Nearly twenty years of progressive damage could be arrested, and possibly some of the five sons of a man mentioned in the introduction could be persuaded to take the pronounced threat of alcohol to their body chemistry seriously in order to avoid the damaging consequences experienced by their alcoholic father.

This all leads to the next question of whether the success of the genetic bioengineers who are splicing, extracting, and recombining genetic material (DNA) from plants, animals, and humans can be focused upon curing the disease of alcoholism. Time will tell.

TWO

Alcoholism Is a Disease

Ethanol, or alcohol, as it is more commonly called, accounted for more than 175,000 deaths in the United States in 1991. Much confusion exists in the public's mind as to whether alcoholism is a disease or, as some feel, a moral issue of willful misconduct or a sign of moral weakness.

My dictionary defines disease as "an unhealthy condition." This definition is certainly encompassing as well as vague. Perhaps this is why there is ongoing debate about the disease concept of alcoholism. The problem of definition is not restricted to alcoholism. Several years ago a significant number of cardiologists, when surveyed, said atherosclerosis, or hardening of the arteries, was not a disease but, rather, an expression of an individual's lifestyle: being overweight, too much fat in the diet, no exercise, smoking, or drinking too much alcohol. Yet medical textbooks devote chapter after chapter to the causes, diagnosis, and complications of this problem, and medical research continues to provide us with ways and means to reduce the number of people exposed to the final consequences of atherosclerosis—death.

So it is with alcoholism. To the clinician working in the field of alcoholism and daily observing the damaging effects of alcohol on the body, the mind, and the spiritual state of individuals from all walks of life, there is no basis for doubting that alcoholism is a disease, as first defined by the American Medical Association in 1956. I, for one, am firmly convinced and most optimistic that medical research and, in turn, increased public awareness will similarly reduce the number of those exposed to the final consequence. To me alcoholism is a disease, irrespective of definitions, semantics, or biases.

Learning the stages of any disease is an elemental step in the practice of medicine. To diagnose and treat a disease, the physician has to learn not only to recognize it but to anticipate what is going to happen next in the disease process. The next step is to find the appropriate treatment to prevent or delay the next stage in the progression. The physician must also be alert to cases in which these things don't happen in the usual way, and recognize many other complications and problems affecting the course of the disease. As an example, let's use measles. When child No. 1 carrying the virus coughs or sneezes into the face of child No. 2 nothing happens for about ten to twelve days (the incubation period). But then child No. 2 starts to have nasal congestion, watery eyes, and all the symptoms of a sore throat or the common cold. About the fourth day, if one looks inside child No. 2's cheeks, one might see what are called Koplik spots, which usually last only twenty-four hours. Next, a rash will appear over the body, and by the seventh or eighth day, a full-blown rash has developed over the entire body. Then it subsides over the next few days. But the physician will have to be alert for complications such as a middle-ear infection, pneumonia, or even encephalitis, any of which can develop. By knowing this sequence of events the physician can effectively treat the disease.

The Disease of Alcoholism

How the disease of alcoholism progresses remains uncertain and controversial. The scientific community has begun to accumulate facts and figures, but the final answer is not yet in place. New information and conceptual breakthroughs will constantly cause us to change and update the model proposed in the next chapter, but for now it serves as a helpful tool in working and learning with our patients.

There are so relatively few unique and specific signs of the early stages of the disease that it has been difficult to develop an accurate working model for this stage. In fact, our guideposts have become focused upon patterns of drinking and the associated behavior—"Is he really drunk, or just tired?"—rather than characteristic physical findings or laboratory tests. It would be helpful if we could just take a chest X-ray as we do to diagnose pneumonia, or an electrocardiogram, as for heart disease. It would be fantastic if we could take one sample of blood and measure some chemical or process unique to the alcoholic. But there is no such test.

Using behavioral characteristics, either by observing the patient or reviewing answers to questionnaires, is complicated by individual variability, and by the limits of interpreting behavior accurately. Patients' drinking patterns and behavior can vary tremendously, just as the drink of choice can range from beer to brandy, especially in the early stages of the disease: "I only drink on the weekend," or "I go on three- to four-day binges where I drink around the clock and then don't touch the stuff for weeks or months." As the later stages come into focus, the drinking patterns become more predictable: "I drink every day," or "I'm starting to drink as soon as I get up in the morning," or "I need an eye opener each morning before I go to work," or "I wake up shaking until I have a drink."

Alcohol

Alcohol is a pharmacologically active chemical. In other words, it's a drug. Just like hundreds of other drugs used in medicine every day, alcohol acts upon different cells in the body and, in fact, acts on different parts of the same cells—such as the cell membrane or different enzymes within the cell—at different rates, causing different effects. People report things like "I take two sips of champagne and my head starts spinning" or "One glass of sherry and I feel warm all over and very relaxed."

Like other drugs used in medicine, the amount of drug taken into the body (the dose) will have different effects— "the first glass or two of wine will make me feel like dancing but after the third or fourth, I'm ready to go to sleep." In general, we can say that alcohol in smaller amounts can be stimulating: appetite increases, the force of the heartbeat is stronger, blood vessels dilate (one begins to feel warm and appear flushed), sex drive and mental alertness seem to increase. Patients report that "After one or two drinks I feel my mind is sharper and I can think more clearly." On the other hand, increasing amounts of alcohol slow down body movement, speech starts to slur, sexual drive is diminished, and sharpness of mind becomes duller and duller. Alcohol is a depressant. An overall depression of body functions begins to take place. One is getting drunk or intoxicated.

Alcohol has been known for years to have the pharmacological properties of an anesthetic agent, just like ether. And when we are exposed to alcohol, or voluntarily drink it, we are anesthetizing ourselves. The alcohol causes certain changes in the chemistry of certain brain cells which result in changes in behavior and physical movement. Anesthesiologists describe four different levels of general anesthesia, but I should emphasize that one level leads to the next in a continuous process and that the boundaries between the levels are really gray.

Level 1—Euphoria

Happy, laughing, singing, general loss of inhibitions, looking at the world through rose-colored glasses, everything is great and all your problems disappear (until the effects wear off). One could ask at this time why patients undergoing surgery don't start singing and dancing and telling jokes in the operating room. The answer, in part, is that the patient is premedicated with sedative-type drugs to minimize this level of anesthesia. One may insist that his primary reason for drinking a particular alcoholic beverage is for the socializing or the taste but, like it or not, in the course of drinking the effects will become evident.

Level II—Amnesia

This level is characterized by an inability to remember what happened in the recent past. Often a patient approached in the recovery room after several hours of surgery will respond to the question, "Joe, how are you doing?" with something like, "Oh, hi, Doc, when are they going to do the surgery?" Little if anything is remembered as to what took place in the operating room. This same level of anesthesia is reached as the dose of alcohol is increased, and is called a blackout.

Level III—Relaxation

This is the point of anesthesia where the muscles of the body are relaxed and the feeling of pain begins to disappear. At this level, the surgeon will proceed with the surgery, and the person drinking alcohol will stagger, fall down, bruise himself, or pass out.

Level IV—Death

Some people feel that you come as close to death as you can without dying when you undergo general anesthesia. As a matter of fact, the major reason alcohol is not used more often as an anesthetic agent is because the dose necessary to bring a person to the relaxation level is very close to the dose that will result in the cessation of breathing and heartbeat. People can and have died from an overdose of alcohol!

Recovery from anesthesia occurs in reverse order. First one regains movement in the arms and legs, overcoming the effects of relaxation; then one begins to feel the pain of the incision or the procedure that was done. The mind begins to clear, and the patient is able to recall the recent past. There may or may not be nausea and vomiting. There does not appear to be a repeat of the euphoric state, most likely because the pain is beginning to dominate the picture.

The person recovering from a heavy bout of drinking undergoes the results of an inevitable chemical aftermath. The alcohol is converted into the toxic chemical acetaldehyde, which may produce the hangover with its nausea, vomiting, sweating, heart palpitations, and usually overshadowing all of these signs, a severe headache.

The Cultural Question

The picture of alcoholism as a disease is further muddied by our society's widespread acceptance of drinking as part of the cultural norm. Statistics indicate that over one hundred million people in the United States alone drink alcoholic beverages: beer, wine, whiskey, wine coolers, champagne, bourbon, rum, scotch, tequila, liqueurs, schnapps, brandy, cognac, vodka, gin, and so on. The use of alcoholic beverages is deeply embedded in the culture of humankind as a rite or celebration. Wine was served at the Last Supper, and with the Passover meal, and worshippers receive wine at the communion rail. Guests toast the bride and groom or a fellow employee at a retirement dinner with champagne.

But why do one hundred million of us drink? Is it the taste of alcoholic beverages? People actually earn a good living deciding whether one wine tastes better than another. And advertisers want us to believe that water from mountain streams used in brewing one brand of beer will give it a better flavor than beer brewed with water from the city supply.

People say, "I enjoy a glass of wine or two with dinner," or "What's a ball game without beer and hotdogs," or "An ice-cold wine cooler on a summer day is a must." Why not a glass of mineral water with dinner, a soda pop with the hotdogs, or ice-cold lemonade on a hot summer day? We all have different taste preferences, just as we have different-colored eyes, hair, and skin. But is it the taste of an alcoholic beverage that we prefer or the effects, or maybe both?

How about thirst? After all, any form of liquid can serve as a thirst quencher, but the contents of the liquid can have other physiological effects on the body that could even be harmful. Remember Dr. Bob's tomato juice? Alcohol is a hygroscopic or dehydrating type of chemical. Alcohol also has a diuretic effect (causing increased urination), resulting in a net loss of body water. A cold beer to quench your thirst after mowing the lawn on a hot summer day will help to cool you off, as well as rehydrate the lining of your throat, at least temporarily. But soon alcohol's dehydrating action will have you thirsting for another one, or looking for a glass of water.

Do we drink mainly for the effects of alcohol? Alcohol can make you feel good all over, relaxed—even help you forget your troubles. But the dose or amount you drink and its effects will vary greatly from person to person, depending on your age, weight, sex, and whether you have an empty or a full stomach, to name a few key variables. However, a more slippery variable in discussing the effects of alcohol is the development of a condition called *tolerance*. This will be discussed in detail, but for now, tolerance is what you get when you have to keep drinking more and more over months or years to get the same effects from drinking.

Culture, religion, taste, thirst, or effects, alcohol is part of all our lives whether we choose to drink or not. Anyone who buys car insurance pays for the effects of drunken drivers, even if he doesn't drink. But to understand the natural history of the disease, we must weigh and sort a mass of confusing social and cultural behaviors and effects to see the underlying process.

National surveys indicate that approximately 10 percent of the one hundred million people who drink alcohol are responsible for purchasing more than half of all the alcoholic beverages sold in the United States. This leads to the question: why do the estimated ten million people who have developed the disease of alcoholism in this country drink primarily for the effects? Chapter 3 suggests some answers.

THREE

A Self-Diagnosis Model: Patterns of Drinking Behavior

The major problem facing the clinician is in diagnosing the disease of alcoholism. Not everyone who drinks alcoholic beverages has the disease of alcoholism. U.S. government reports indicate that 10.5 million Americans are alcoholics, with another 76 million affected either directly or indirectly by alcohol abuse.

The problem is further complicated by the fact that alcohol, as noted in the previous chapter, is an anesthetic drug and any person who drinks enough alcohol can be anesthetized or intoxicated. As a rule of thumb, it is estimated that one out of every ten people who drink alcoholic beverages is either an alcoholic or will develop the disease if they continue to drink alcoholic beverages. Thus, in any setting where there are approximately one hundred people, be it in church, temple, office, plant, classroom, statistically ten people are alcoholics or will become alcoholics if they continue to drink. As the saying goes, "It can happen to anyone." These ten individuals have become addicted or could become addicted to alcohol: they have developed a compulsive behavior to drink, even though this behavior causes physical and emotional harm to themselves as well as those around them. They have lost control.

Alcohol, or more precisely, its breakdown product acetaldehyde, is also potentially toxic to all body organs, depending upon the concentration (how much alcohol consumed over what period of time). The challenge in recognizing the signs of alcoholism is not to confuse the three biological effects of alcohol: (1) anesthetic (intoxicating) effects, (2) addictive effects, and (3) toxic effects.

The field of medicine, like any other discipline, has its "lumpers" and its "splitters." The lumpers tend to deal with the larger groups of whatever is being classified, and the splitters try to break things down into smaller and smaller distinct groups. I am a lumper. It follows, then, that my proposed patterns or stages that occur in the development of alcoholism are generalizations. Models with much more detailed behavioral patterns of drinking during the progression and recovery phases of the disease were described many years ago. What I hope to do is provide enough detail in this working model to allow anyone reading this book to be able to classify himself (a self-diagnosis), or to make an educated guess about a relative's or friend's pattern of drinking.

Exposure-to-Alcohol Stage

Estimates from various surveys lead us to believe that approximately 30 percent of Americans insist that they have never touched a drop of alcohol in their lives. In all likelihood, they never have taken a drink of an alcoholic beverage knowingly, but they were probably exposed to the molecules of alcohol at some time. Why? Because of such practices as whiskey on the gums for teething, hidden alcohols in foods, medicines, and over-the-counter remedies, and possibly even because of exposure during gestation. I think it is more realistic to conclude that something like 99.9 percent of Americans have been exposed to alcohol at some time in their life. Here's why.

During Gestation

The most unfortunate and perhaps the most dramatic exposure to alcohol is prenatal. A baby born to a mother who drank a significant amount during pregnancy may have a small head; flattening of the face, including a pushed-up pug nose; and a dullness of facial expression rather than responsive smiles or gurgles. Evidence of mental retardation may increase as the baby grows. These various symptoms in a newborn are referred to as fetal alcohol syndrome. It was recently found that the brains of newborn rats can become damaged if alcohol is fed to the mother during pregnancy. This syndrome, like the disease of alcoholism, did not suddenly appear on the scene but is becoming more widely recognized as physicians look for it. We can even find evidence of it in eighteenth-century painting. For instance, *Gin Lane*, by English painter William Hogarth, shows a London scene during the so-called Gin Epidemic in which a woman in the crowd, obviously drunk, has just delivered a baby on the bank of the River Thames. Careful examination of the painting reveals that the baby's face strongly suggests the features of fetal alcohol syndrome.

There is still much to be learned about the effects of

alcohol upon the developing fetus. The physician taking care of a pregnant woman is usually placed in a difficult position when asked, "Do I have to stop drinking completely? I thought a glass of wine each day would be good for me; at least, that's what my grandmother told me." At this point, the dose or amount of alcohol that would harm the developing baby is not known and undoubtedly varies from person to person. But why take a chance? Just stop drinking (and smoking cigarettes for that matter) during pregnancy! Easier said than done for a woman who is physically dependent upon alcohol, and a tremendous dilemma for the physician caring for her. But that is a topic for another book.

What about the baby whose mother drank during pregnancy but who appears to be perfectly normal at birth? Will this person be more susceptible to developing alcoholism in adult life? It is not uncommon to see the newborn baby of a mother dependent upon certain drugs during pregnancy go through a typical withdrawal from the drug shortly after birth. The evidence is not clear-cut where alcohol is involved. However, since research has shown that alcohol can cross the placenta, it seems reasonable to conclude that it could affect the developing fetus in ways as yet unknown.

Hidden Alcohols

If you haven't already tried this, please do. Go to the local drug store or supermarket pharmacy section and start reading the content labels of different cough syrups, decongestant syrups, liquid pain-killer medicines, and literally hundreds of over-the-counter liquid preparations, including mouthwashes. You will learn that essentially all of them contain alcohol in concentrations ranging from 10 to 15 percent (20 to 30 proof). You might be surprised when you read on the label of a product advertised on television as a sure way to get a good night's sleep that it has an alcohol content of 25 percent (50 proof). Even more interesting is the fact that the label, until recently, did not give the percentage of alcohol concentration, but only the statement: "Warning, this product contains alcohol." Another product that sponsored a favorite weekly musical television show for years (its theme was, ironically, "champagne music") once contained 35 percent (70 proof) alcohol; has since been reduced to 12 percent (24 proof), still more than that of an average table wine.

What is the significance of these hidden alcohols? First, it suggests that just about everyone has been exposed to alcohol at some time, whether he realizes it or not. Second, that the first exposure probably occurred very early in life, since many liquid medicines commonly given to babies and infants are included in the group with alcohol levels ranging from 10 to 15 percent (20 to 30 proof).

One might argue that only very small doses were given, but certain studies carried out on newborn laboratory animals give cause for reflection. If a newborn female mouse or rat is injected with tiny amounts of the female sex hormone estrogen prior to three days of age, at least two very important things will happen: (1) the subject will grow up to be a perfectly normal-sized animal and (2) *it will be sterile*, that is, it will be unable to reproduce because of a disturbance between the part of the brain called the hypothalamus and the pituitary gland.

However, if the same dose of estrogen is injected *after* four days of age, the subject will not only grow up to be a normal-sized animal, but it will be able to reproduce normal offspring.

Scientific evidence continues to accumulate that if animals and humans are exposed to certain chemicals during the early stages of growth and development, changes can occur in the body that will not show up until adulthood. Each time I give this talk, I raise this controversial, but certainly provocative, question: "Are we all here today talking about alcoholism because we were exposed to one or more of the hidden alcohols when we were babies?" I don't know the answer, but I find it encouraging to see certain pharmaceutical companies advertising one of their baby medicines as containing no aspirin, no sugar, and no alcohol.

The Curiosity Drinker Stage

I often hear statements like the following:

"My grandfather made his own wine, and he always offered me a little sip."

"I used to sneak drinks at my parents' parties after everyone left."

"My school friends would come over and we would raid the liquor cabinet."

"My older brother would buy us a few six-packs, and we would go out to the lake for a party."

"Our crowd started drinking beer because pot was getting too expensive."

"A birthday party wasn't a party during my high school days unless they served drinks."

In general, this phase represents part of the testing and experimenting teenage years. The motivation for drinking would appear to be a combination of social (peer pressure) customs, taste, and the effects. Perhaps the greater emphasis is on acceptance and adventure, but unintentional results may include problems with parents, school, and even the law. It is also possible that the first taste of alcohol proved very distasteful ("burned my throat"), or that the first hangover was so convincing that the person never drank alcohol again.

The Nondrinker Stage

The phase of *nondrinking* can occur at any point in one's life. Some people, indeed, have never voluntarily taken a drink. This may have resulted from certain moral or religious standards in their homes while they were growing up: "Alcohol was never permitted in our home" or "Dad would kill me if I ever took a drink." Possibly they tried alcohol once (curiosity phase) and didn't like it. They report that "I couldn't stand the taste so I never tried it again" or "I got drunk one time in high school and was so sick I never tried it again" or "I saw the misery caused by my Dad's drinking and I never touched a drop."

There is also a large group of people who, as a result of developing the disease of alcoholism and as part of their recovery, completely abstain from any type of alcoholic beverage. Unlike the nondrinkers described above, they are vulnerable to having a relapse of their disease if they take that "first drink."

The Social Drinker Stage

Everyone who drinks alcohol claims at one time or another, "Yes, I drink, but I'm only a social drinker." Some have attempted to define the social drinker on the basis of the amount one drinks: "I usually have a glass of wine with dinner"; "I have one or two glasses of beer and then I quit"; "A half-glass of wine and I feel tipsy."

Rather than attempting to define the social drinker now, it might be more pertinent to ask why 100 million people drink alcoholic beverages. I believe people drink alcohol for at least four reasons:

1. Custom, tradition, or as a symbol of celebration.
2. Taste (for those who find it appealing).
3. Thirst, as one seeks a tall, cool drink on a hot summer day (despite the dehydrating and diuretic effects of alcohol mentioned earlier).
4. The anesthetic effects of alcohol—one feels more relaxed, less anxious, and begins to see life through rose-colored glasses.

The effects of alcohol may increase with certain psychological and/or physical conditions in the body—one may be very fatigued, very anxious, or have an empty stomach. In some people the feeling of euphoria seems to register in their memory banks, and at some point, they may find themselves seeking alcohol to gain that euphoric effect with the mistaken notion that it will somehow assist them over a rough period in living. However, the key feature under all of these circumstances for the social drinker is that he recognizes the effects and stops. "No, thank you, I've had enough!" The individual has maintained the capacity for control and may remain at this phase for the rest of his life.

The Impulsive Drinker Stage

This group probably represents the majority of people who drink alcoholic beverages. Unlike the social drinker, who drinks primarily as a custom and for taste, and unlike the recreational drinker described below, who intentionally drinks for the effects, the impulsive drinker falls somewhere in between. This is the person who would normally be considered a social drinker but on an impulse will begin to drink for the effects—at weddings, birthdays, anniversaries, promotions, over stressful problems at home or work, broken love affairs, financial crises, and so forth. But these impulsive episodes are usually self-limiting. Frequently, the individual will experience the symptoms of the morning-after hangover and promise everyone, including God, that "I'll never touch another drop!" This period of abstinence may last several hours, days, weeks, years, or even a lifetime. However, the individual will more likely follow a cyclical pattern of social drinking, impulsive drinking (including hangover), abstinence or nondrinking, and back to social drinking. This pattern may be lifelong.

The Addictive Drinker Stage

At any time in life, it is possible for the social and impulsive drinker to enter the addictive stage of drinking behavior. The individual develops a compulsive behavior to drink to obtain a mood-altering effect from the alcohol in spite of the physical and psychological problems he or she may be imposing on him or herself and on those around them. The addictive stage includes three types of drinking behavior.

The Recreational Drinker

At this point the focus is on the drink and the effects it has to offer. Drinking becomes as much a part of having fun as playing ball or any other sport. One is drinking to win, or more appropriately, drinking for an effect. There is a goal and a purpose: feeling good and having fun. The popular T.G.I.F. (Thank God It's Friday) crowds, or "happy hours" at local bars and taverns, are a major part of the recreational drinker's game. This is seen more often than not on college campuses on the weekends.

Recently I became involved in a case where the patient was a first-year college student who had joined a fraternity and lived in the fraternity house. One Sunday morning he woke up and began to vomit blood. He was rushed to the student infirmary. His symptoms looked very much like those of a bleeding peptic ulcer. However, putting together the history of the weekend, along with the physical examination, it came to light that the fraternity house ordered a keg of beer each Friday night whether there was a party or not. This young patient became involved in a game of ping pong wherein if you lost or won a point—I never did find out the rules of the game—you had to chug-a-lug a glass of beer. It turns out that he had consumed between 19 and 22 beers during the night—he was either a great ping pong player or a very poor one—and this brought about an acute gastritis, or irritation to his stomach lining, which was the source of the bleeding. What was supposed to be fun could have turned into a disaster. I should emphasize that one need not go to college to become involved in this type of drinking behavior; it can take place any time and any place that alcoholic beverages are available.

However, two very important lessons are learned during this stage: (1) alcohol can make you very sick, i.e., the common hangover, and (2) alcohol can make you temporarily forget your troubles and become generally euphoric or happy.

For some, the hangover experience is usually a short-lived memory; the next weekend the whole sequence is repeated. In others, one hangover can lead to a lifelong aversion to alcohol and total abstinence.

Psychologically Dependent Drinker Stage

The person who has learned to seek out alcohol for its euphoric or sedative effects comes to depend upon it psychologically, if not physically. Individuals found in this group are experiencing pain—physical pain, like that of arthritis ("None of the medicine my doctor gives me for my arthritis works; the only time I don't feel the pain is when I drink")—or the pain of being unable to cope with the stresses and strains of life's circumstances ("Doc, I'm so lonely, I only have my dogs and my beer"). Alcohol is viewed as the means to relieve the pain. Whether the pain is the constant throbbing ache of arthritis, cancer, heart disease, or feelings of hopelessness from marital or financial problems, loss of a job, or any of an endless list of problems, this group will start drinking more and more to get the desired effects of alcohol to assist them in dealing with their distress. This is a form of self-medication. Some people will take tranquilizers, with or without a doctor's prescription, while others will recognize that alcohol gives them the same euphoric and sedative effects in less time than seeing a doctor and getting a prescription filled. As one patient remarked when I was discussing this type of drinker: "Hey Doc, it *is* cheaper than going to a doctor's office. First you'll be charged for the office visit and then you have to pay for a prescription. Heck, for a few dollars I can buy a bottle and get the same effect."

This patient is absolutely correct, except that he is not taking into account the numerous consequences that go along with that bottle.

It is at this point that we begin to see the problem of the dual diagnosis or the dual disease syndrome. The drinker may also have some type of emotional problem. The diagnosis can range from anxiety disorder to psychosis such as schizophrenia, manic-depressive illness, or major depression. Other drinkers can have an organic brain disorder or some other form of dementia and find that alcohol serves as a temporary fix by quieting them down. After a while a dependency develops, and whenever there is anxiety or agitation the individual looks to alcohol for relief. More about the dual diagnosis later.

Extremes of this type of drinker range from the person who has to stop off at the local bar for a few drinks each day in order to face problems at home ("The car won't run," "Johnny needs braces," or "The furnace will cost $1,000") to the patient who tells me, "Doc, I can't go to bed at night unless I have a bottle of wine to put me to sleep." Upon awakening in the morning, he may find the bottle empty, or half empty.

Furthermore, a high percentage of the homeless "street people" and extremely poor people in general may well reach this phase of alcoholism. For some it probably requires a daily numbing with alcohol to deal with their condition.

Compulsive Drinker Stage

This stage is a controversial subject, because it is difficult for someone who can say "I made up my mind, I'm not going to drink any more" and follow through to understand, or even believe, someone who says "I can't stop drinking." We readily recognize the addictive power of drugs like heroin, morphine, amphetamines, and cocaine. We often blame the substance, not the addict. But our society has tended to view alcohol in a different light, possibly because although it is so widely used, only a percentage of those who drink become alcoholics. We may make moral judgments when we see a person vomit up the last drink as fast as he or she swallows it and still go back for more.

Some refer to the compulsive drinker as the pure alcoholic, and believe the pure alcoholic is becoming extinct as more and more people develop multiple or cross addictions to what alcoholics call dry drugs.

Although a detailed discussion of addiction is outside the boundaries of this book, some general comments are in order at this time. Definitions of addiction can be confusing and contradictory, depending upon one's biases and perspective. I find myself attracted to a definition proposed by Dr. A. Goldstein: "Addiction is the compulsive, self-destructive, chronic self-administration of a mood-altering drug. Addiction is a *behavior*, and like all behavior, it has a chemical basis in the brain."

Two physical changes *may* or *may not* occur in the compulsive drinker, or, for that matter, in the psychologically dependent or recreational drinker as we have defined them. The first is the need to increase the amount of alcohol one needs to get the desired effects (tolerance), and the second is symptoms of sweating, shaking, rapid heart rate, or diarrhea when one suddenly stops drinking (withdrawal associated with physical dependence). One who is addicted to a certain chemical will usually develop tolerance to that chemical, but will not necessarily become physically dependent on the substance. Our working model holds that the psychologically dependent drinker, the recreational drinker, and the compulsive drinker are all addicted to alcohol. Whether or not they will cross the line and become physically dependent upon alcohol cannot be predicted with any laboratory tests available today. They will know they have crossed the line only when it has happened.

What causes addiction, whether to alcohol or to drugs, remains unknown, but scientists are actively seeking out a chemical basis for this type of behavior. Studies on experimental animals are beginning to shed some light on this subject. Experimenters have placed fine, needle-sized tubes in different parts of the animals' brains. These tubes are connected to a reservoir of fluid that can contain different types of drugs. By pressing a bar-lever, the animals can deliver a small amount of drug to the region of the brain where the needle-like tube is located.

These types of studies have revealed at least two very important concepts: (1) all behavior has a chemical basis in the brain, i.e, changes in our moods and behavior are due to changes in the brain's chemistry, and (2) there is a specific region of the brain called the primary reward center; when stimulated, whether in animals or humans, by eating (hunger), drinking (thirst), or procreation (sex), a positive reinforcing effect will occur, that is, the animal will repeat the behavior again and again for the presumably pleasurable experience. The latter behavior is found in all living creatures with a brain, be it cricket, fish, frog, bird, monkey, or man. Why? To survive.

In these experimental settings, the animals learn that pressing a bar-lever will reward them with an injection of a certain "mood-altering" drug. They soon reach the point where they develop a compulsive pattern of hitting the bar-lever to self-administer the drug again and again. The studies with cocaine are most dramatic. The animal will start pressing the bar-lever to deliver an injection of cocaine to the "reward center," and the craving apparently becomes so great that the animal will keep pressing and pressing the bar-lever until it actually kills itself from cocaine overdose. I recall this type of study every time one of my patients says, "Doc, I take one drink and I can't stop."

I should emphasize that the animals will compulsively self-administer the same drugs that humans can become addicted to and compulsively self-administer, but that, very importantly, neither animals nor humans will become addicted to or compulsively self-administer most other kinds of drugs, including aspirin, digitalis, and insulin. Not even drugs that act primarily on the brain, like haloperidol (Haldol), lithium, or antidepressants produce this compulsive type of behavior.

The results obtained when alcohol was placed in the reservoir and delivered to the same region of the brain when the animal pressed the lever were not as dramatic as with cocaine. It appeared that the animal would hit the lever only occasionally. However, when acetaldehyde (the first chemical by-product of alcohol as it is broken down in the liver) was placed in the reservoir, the animal began to press the lever more frequently. These studies suggest that alcohol itself is not the addicting chemical, but rather the breakdown product of alcohol, acetaldehyde.

This finding corroborates the reports of those who say that once they start drinking alcohol, they can't stop, or as the expression goes in AA circles, "they lost control." Exciting ongoing research on the chemistry of the brain and how it works will undoubtably provide us with a much clearer picture of this type of behavior.

The Physically Dependent Drinker Stage or Crossing the Line

The transition between the psychologically dependent, compulsive, or recreational drinker to a state of physical dependency on alcohol does not appear to be a sudden and abrupt event, but rather a gradual process with the duration varying from person to person. Physical dependency tends to creep up on you until it is too late and the line has been crossed. To understand this transition a little better, let's deal with physical dependency first and then talk about crossing the line.

Up until the physical dependency phase, the preceding stages tend to blend into one another and, as suggested above, there is a reversibility of the process. That is, one can decide to quit one day and there are minimal physical consequences in terms of pain and discomfort. However, once the line is crossed into physical dependence, one starts to experience all the physical and emotional discomforts of withdrawal from alcohol when one stops drinking. As noted earlier, physical dependence on alcohol is a complication of addiction. One type of drinker can be emotionally addicted to alcohol—abuse it frequently or infrequently—but, for whatever chemical reason, the person may never become physically dependent upon alcohol.

How do you know whether you are physically dependent on alcohol? The simplest test is to stop drinking: if anywhere from three to twelve hours after your last drink you start experiencing a series of physical and emotional signs and symptoms, then you are clearly physically dependent. What are these signs and symptoms?

Initially, patients report that they experience an internal shaking sensation. Since these "shakes" cannot be seen by an examiner, one is dependent on the individual for a description. Descriptions I've heard range from "It feels like my stomach is in knots" to an extreme "It feels like I'd imagine it would if I swallowed a hand grenade and it exploded inside of me."

If the blood alcohol level continues to fall (that is, the person doesn't take a drink) the next experience is tremors. The hands and certain facial muscles can shake rather violently, at times so much that a person cannot pick up a cup of coffee or feed himself. These are called intentional tremors in that if the person puts his hands in his pockets or rests them in his lap, the tremors tend to disappear or reduce in intensity. However, if he tries to do some deliberate type of movement with the hands, the tremors reappear. People have been known to hide their drinking problem for years because as soon as they start experiencing these tremors, they take a drink of alcohol, increase their blood alcohol level, and the tremors disappear. Recently, I had a salesperson wait on me at a local department store. As she started to write up the bill, her hands began to shake so badly that she dropped the pencil several times. She excused herself to "look something up," returned a few minutes later, and began to write the order with no trouble. Although the odor of perfume was somewhat overpowering, the smell of whatever she had drunk was easily noticed. She had had her fix of alcohol and was functioning again.

Similarly, I have talked with AA members who go out on what are called "Twelve-step calls." The twelfth and final step of the AA program is to share what you have learned with others. When someone with a drinking problem sends out a call for help, members who are "working the twelfth step" respond. They tell me that as a matter of practice, they take along a bottle of gin or a six-pack of beer. When they arrive on the scene and the person in need of help has already started into withdrawal, particularly tremors, they give them several drinks to calm them down—restore their blood alcohol level—and then bring them into the treatment center for detoxification.

As the blood alcohol level continues to fall, the next symptom to appear, after the tremors, is hallucinations; the person undergoing detoxification will start to hear and see things that don't exist. Again, it is not possible to see any evidence, so one depends upon the patient for descriptions.

One thing that characterizes people experiencing hallucinations is that they are obviously frightened and apprehensive. One patient insisted five or six times one night that he saw a mongoose running down the hospital corridor. He had never read Kipling's *Riki-Tiki-Tavi*, so I'm not certain how he recognized a mongoose.

Following the hallucinations, one may experience seizures or convulsions. These are sometimes referred to as rum fits and cannot always be distinguished from a grand mal epileptic seizure. Not all seizures related to alcohol occur only when one has stopped drinking and is going into withdrawal. Certain persons who are drinking large quantities of alcoholic beverages may have a seizure when their blood alcohol level is rising and apparently exceeding what may be referred to as the seizure threshold of the brain.

The withdrawal seizures themselves are usually self-limited and, with proper attention to keeping an open airway and getting the person to lie down on the floor so he or she can't fall out of bed, are not life-threatening. But they are certainly frightening. The dangerous aspect of having a seizure is that it may occur at an unexpected time. If you are driving your car when one of these seizures begins, the consequences are scary to say the least. Not only could you harm yourself, but other people as well. I feel very strongly that one should go through withdrawal from alcohol in a medically staffed facility trained to deal with these types of complications. Although there are those who relate how they went cold turkey to get off the alcohol, I feel this is potentially very dangerous.

Doctors have been debating about whether a person who has a seizure should be started on an antiseizure medication such as Dilantin, which is very effective in controlling epileptic seizures. There is a growing consensus that Dilantin is ineffective in controlling alcohol-related seizures, although some emergency-room physicians routinely send patients who have had an alcohol-withdrawal seizure home on Dilantin with instructions to stay on the medication indefinitely. As a result, we sometimes have a patient admitted to our treatment center with a history of seizures despite taking Dilantin. Sometimes it is not possible to determine by history whether one has had epileptic seizures or alcohol-related seizures. We then do a diagnostic workup including an electroencephalogram of the brain waves and a CAT scan of the brain to rule out any evidence of epilepsy or brain tumor. If the results come back within normal limits, we usually discontinue the Dilantin. I hasten to add that there are some individuals who have epileptic seizures and who have a problem with alcohol. In these instances, we treat both diseases: the epilepsy and the alcoholism.

Finally, as the blood alcohol level continues to fall, the person may go into *delirium tremens* or the D.T.'s. This condition is characterized by all of the symptoms I've just described. Patients in D.T.'s can have tremors, hallucinations, and seizures but, in addition, can go into shock and a total disruption of the autonomic nervous system that can result in irregular heart beats, severe gastrointestinal distress with nausea, vomiting, belly cramps, and diarrhea. Most important, these individuals are so out of it that they may do great harm to themselves. The mortality rate of people who develop D.T.'s can be as high as 25 percent. When compared to the mortality rate of coronary by-pass surgery (about 2 to 3 percent), it should be evident that the D.T.'s have very serious consequences. The "cold turkey" approach is extremely risky and should be avoided at all costs.

One can similarly cross the line to physical dependency when abusing the so-called dry sedatives like Valium, Librium, Ativan, Serax, Xanax, Tranxene, or phenobarbitol. It is interesting to compare the similarities and differences in the withdrawal process between alcohol and these sedatives. It is sometimes said that Valium is nothing more than dehydrated gin. The sedative addict goes through a withdrawal process very similar to that of the person coming off alcohol. The major differences are that with dry drugs the first signs of withdrawal will not occur until three to four *days* after the last pill, as compared to alcohol withdrawal, which starts in three to four hours after the last drink. The length of withdrawal is about seven to ten days for dry drugs, whereas it takes three to five days to withdraw from alcohol.

This time difference can be of vital importance when treating the patient during withdrawal, as we experienced with one of our patients. Mary was a fifty-four-year-old former nurse when we admitted her to our eight-day acute treatment program. She was in moderate to severe withdrawal, with severe tremors and reported hallucinations. She admitted to drinking about a fifth of vodka every day for the past several months or so. She responded well to our treatment, which included a dose schedule for Librium for four days. By day five she was free of any withdrawal signs or symptoms. On the evening of her seventh day in the center, she was saying her goodbyes and was in excellent spirits. Suddenly, she had a seizure lasting approximately one minute and became very frightened and apprehensive. We did diagnostic testing for a seizure disorder. All tests were reported as normal. It was only at that time that the patient revealed that she had been taking about 50 mg of Librium daily for the past year or so. Even though her drug screen on admission had showed near-toxic levels of Librium in her blood, we had attributed it to her admission history. She said she had been taking some Librium to deal with the tremors occurring when she decided to go cold turkey from alcohol and became frightened. The moral of this case is that one must be on the alert for cross-dependency between alcohol and other sedatives, and to the delayed onset of withdrawal symptoms when dealing with the dry sedatives. In fact, the clinical course of Mary's case suggests that she went through alcohol withdrawal first and Librium withdrawal immediately afterwards. There was no way one could prove this at the time, but it has put us on the alert for similar types of cases.

How do we treat the withdrawal from alcohol? I like to use the coiled-spring model which, although oversimplified, appears to provide patients with a better understanding of what is happening in their bodies when they stop drinking. Imagine the nervous system of the body as a powerful coiled spring; its lengthening and shortening reflect the ups and downs of our everyday living. Some days we feel on top of the world, others, we feel down and depressed. When we consume significant quantities of alcohol, it tends to suppress this movement, as we might do when we get very anxious—we compress the spring tightly and "hold it in." Continuing to drink keeps tightening the spring and constricting it further until it is greatly reduced in length and tightly coiled. Only by keeping a certain alcohol level do we maintain a level of reduced anxiety, particularly if we are physically dependent on alcohol. The nervous system is artificially held down with alcohol. Then we stop drinking and all of this energy in the spring is released; it overshoots its normal functioning state, causing all sorts of physiological disruption in the body like tremors, palpitations of the heart, diarrhea, loss of appetite, internal shaking, depression, and just plain feeling sick. With the use of a sedative like Librium, the jangling spring (the nervous system) is brought under control again with a decreasing dose schedule ending on the fourth day after admission.

Because of variation in individual responses to Librium, as well as the different degrees of liver injury secondary to the alcohol, the amount of Librium we give has to be adjusted up or down on an individualized basis. Sometimes it is necessary to give as much as 600mg of Librium in six hours when dealing with patients in severe withdrawal. Someone with liver damage may start accumulating the Librium because the liver has lost some of its capacity to metabolize or break down the drug, and the patient becomes very sleepy and has a sensation of his legs going out from under him. This is a form of Librium intoxication. My main point in bringing this matter up is that some patients will obtain Librium through various means and try to detox themselves. Recently, there has been much talk about detoxing on an outpatient basis, arguing that patients do not have to be hospitalized when going through withdrawal. I strongly feel, about either of these approaches, that withdrawal treatment has to be carefully individualized and I believe this can only be done safely under constant monitoring of the patient's clinical status during the whole withdrawal phase.

Because of what I have learned about the complications of

the withdrawal process, I am seriously concerned over the position increasingly taken by both governmental and private insurance agencies who have established policies that they will only pay for a three-day detox treatment. Again and again, we have treated patients who were physically unstable for six to seven days after admission, while some talked of going home after the first two days of treatment. Everyone's reactions to drugs and alcohol are highly individualized, and there should be more latitude to take that tremendous variation into account. I feel the main focus of any of these policies should be to bring the patient safely through the detoxification phase and into an effective, long-term treatment plan. Better still, the same resources and energy should go into policies that prevent the progression of the disease, such as early education and alcohol information, group therapy, individual counseling, lectures, movies, AA members' visits, and AA meetings.

FOUR

Crossing the Line to Physical Dependence

Old-timers in AA view the gradual transition into physical dependence on alcohol with an analogy: "When does a cucumber become a pickle? Does it become a pickle the minute it is taken from the vine and placed in the pickling solution? No, it will still taste like a cucumber. But with time, it will taste more and more like a pickle, until everyone agrees that this is a pickle and not a cucumber." The same is true when one becomes physically dependent on alcohol. Early symptoms of withdrawal—irritability, sleeplessness, and generalized anxiety—progress to the later signs of waking up in the morning with the shakes. Most importantly, all of these signs and symptoms can be relieved with another drink. As the shakes increase in intensity, only repeated drinks, about every three to four hours, will keep them under control. One who is physically dependent on alcohol will know it when it happens. His life begins to focus more and more on the next drink and everything else takes second place. As one patient recently told me, "I need to drink three fishbowls (16 oz.) of beer each morning before I can legibly write my name, and then a fifth of whiskey during the rest of the day keeps me going."

After listening to literally thousands of patients who have become physically dependent on alcohol and who have experienced the physical and emotional sufferings of the withdrawal syndrome, certain patterns in their social and medical histories began to appear consistently. We could also see some of the same social and medical patterns in patients who had not yet crossed the line into physical dependency. It occurred to us that these patterns might be useful in helping predict whether or not someone else was in the process of crossing the line. So, the following list of social and medical problems are warning signs:

Warning Signs

1. Dependence on cigarette smoking.

Only six out of more than 5,000 patients admitted to Ignatia Hall in the past ten years say they have never smoked a cigarette. In general, nearly all of our patients report that the number of packs they regularly smoke is almost directly related to the amount of alcohol normally consumed. When I ask, "Would you be able to go to sleep at home tonight if you knew there wasn't a pack of cigarettes in the house?" invariably about 90 percent of the group will answer "No way!" Patients also report that "When I drink, I smoke more," which can be compared to another frequently heard statement, "I don't eat when I drink." It is difficult not to speculate that a person physically dependent on one chemical is more prone to become dependent on other chemicals.

Contrary to popular opinion, the nicotine in tobacco products is proving to be the gateway drug to alcohol abuse and addiction rather than smoking marijuana.

2. Experiencing blackouts.

Blackouts are short-term amnesia, or a temporary loss of memory. One extreme example might illustrate this condition. A patient called from Cleveland, Ohio, one Thanksgiving morning and asked if a bed was available. There was, so he said that he would arrive in Akron about 4:00 P.M. He did not get there until 10:00 P.M., but this was not a problem. Three days later we received a telephone call from his mother in Youngstown, Ohio, inquiring about her son, because she had learned he was in a hospital. Since he had spent Thanksgiving Day with his parents and relatives and seemed happy and normal, the mother assumed he must have been in a car accident. In compliance with federal guidelines not to reveal the presence of any patient in our center unless the patient gives his or her permission, I went to the patient and asked for his consent to acknowledge his presence to his mother. It was indeed a surprise when the patient responded, "Doc, I haven't seen my parents in five years!" That's a blackout!

This is an extreme case, but more common examples heard in our center include:

"Many times I don't remember how I got home or, better still, how I got into bed."

"It seems like every time I drink, I lose my car; I can't remember where I parked it."

"I keep losing papers at work, or I forget to keep appointments."

"Sometimes I don't remember going to work, or what I did at work until I get home."

Over 85 percent of our patients have experienced blackouts, and to us this is one of the top predictors of crossing the line.

3. Divorce(s).

Approximately 50 percent of our patients have been divorced one or more times because of their drinking problem. A significant number of those patients who are divorced remarried alcoholics. On the other hand, half of our patients have remained married to the same spouse in spite of numerous relapses and more than one treatment program. Why some spouses will stick it out through thick and thin and others will take the route of divorce is unknown. I have been impressed with the number of nondrinking wives who will be so supportive of their husbands that they, in effect, help perpetuate the drinking problem. AA calls this enabling, and those who do it are enablers. An example of enabling would be calling the boss and telling him or her that your spouse is sick with the flu when the spouse really has a hangover.

4. Attending an AA meeting prior to entering a treatment program.

Approximately 60 percent of our patients have attended an Alcoholics Anonymous meeting at some time before being admitted for their first alcoholism treatment. In general, these patients did not follow up with the AA program, but the significant point is that they were at least suspicious that they might have an alcohol problem.

5. Attempts to stop drinking—abstinence.

Approximately 40 percent of our patients report that they had made attempts to stop drinking at some time prior to being admitted for their first treatment. The period of abstinence varies from a few days to a couple of weeks to several months. Again, the actual time period is not as important as the fact that the attempt was made, which indicated a suspicion or recognition that they were in trouble with alcohol.

6. Use of illicit drugs.

AA members are beginning to speculate that the "pure alcoholic" is becoming extinct. The trend among the younger patients admitted to our center (twenty to thirty years of age) is more and more in the direction of poly-substance abuse: alcohol with marijuana, speed (amphetamines) and cocaine, as well as prescription drugs like Valium, Librium, and barbiturates. We find that at least 80 percent of our patients under the age of thirty give a history of using marijuana or speed at some time in their lives, usually starting in high school. About 20 percent of these patients are still using marijuana on a fairly regular basis at the time of admission. Apparently, the use of alcohol gained prominence in their lives because of the legal risks associated with marijuana, as well as financial considerations.

Cocaine users have an interesting problem. Simply stated, they get high on coke and come down with alcohol. In spite of this trend toward cross-addiction, we still find that 90 percent or more of our patients of any age group give a history consistent with the diagnosis of alcoholism. Laboratory tests, including drug testing, are consistent with this diagnosis.

However, despite the rising trend of cross-addiction in our younger patient population, patients over forty, on their first admission to our unit, tend to respond emphatically to the question "Have you ever used street drugs?" Their answers range from an indignant "No, sir! Never!" or "Alcohol is bad enough!" to "What do you take me for, a drug addict?" The point is that the standards of behavior in our society are changing, and with them our addictive practices. What was considered wrong in one generation is apparently acceptable to another.

These changing behavior standards, plus increasing scientific evidence for a chemical basis of behavior, have created a real problem in the treatment of alcoholism. The trend has been to eliminate any distinction between alcohol abuse and drug abuse and lump them together as the problems of chemical dependency. Although the basic biochemical mechanism in terms of brain chemistry may be the same, there is a distinct attitudinal difference between the two groups, as well as cultural differences, differences in medical complications, and some not-to-be-overlooked legal differences. The drug users tend to look down their noses at the alcohol users, and this can create a great deal of friction disruptive to the overall treatment program. However, through the educational and persuasive efforts of the staff, each patient can begin to accept the similarity of an addictive behavior, whether his or her chemical of choice is alcohol, cocaine, marijuana, prescription sedatives and tranquilizers, or street drugs.

I find it interesting and even historically significant that one of the co-founders of AA (Dr. Bob) was dependent upon barbiturates as well as alcohol. Using drugs in addition to alcohol is a warning sign.

7. Arrests for alcohol-related offenses.

About 70 percent of our first-admission patients report that they have been arrested one or more times for some

alcohol-related offense: public intoxication, disorderly conduct, domestic violence, DWI (driving while intoxicated), or
DUI (driving under the influence). Because of new state
laws, the number of people admitted to our treatment center
because of a court order is increasing. In addition to giving
out jail sentences, courts are also ordering many offenders
into alcoholism treatment programs. As might be suspected,
the major alcohol-related offense is the DWI. Almost 30
percent of our first-admission patients over the age of thirty-
five years report from one to eight DWIs, with the first one
most likely to occur in the late teenage period (eighteen to
twenty-one years). Statisticians tell us that the probability of
a person drinking to reach a blood alcohol level of 0.10
percent or 100 mg/dl (that is to say, legally intoxicated) and
then driving a car *and* being arrested by police are relatively
low. The odds cited are between 300 and 500 to 1. Most
people who have received a DWI or DUI give us the
message that drinking and driving has been a relatively
common practice. As with any chance occurrence, receiving
a DWI or DUI might be a fluke or unusual circumstance,
but to us, such arrests are very suggestive of early warning
signs in the development of alcoholism and deserves more
attention in diagnosis and in future research.

8. Fired or warned on the job.

Less than 10 percent of our first-time admissions report
that they had been either fired or warned about their job
because of alcohol. Another 10 percent or so will state that
although they were never fired or warned, they would quit
or resign before they were fired. Relatively few were sum-
marily discharged for drinking on the job, but rather were
warned or fired because of absenteeism. They failed to show

up for work because they were either too sick with a hangover or were still out drinking. I have been impressed with the
attitude of the larger corporations in our area who have
acknowledged the existence of the disease of alcoholism. As
in dealing with other employees with chronic illnesses, they
are, in the main, very supportive of their employees seeking
treatment. On a recent visit to Germany, I was impressed
with the fact that at several of the alcohol treatment centers I
visited, almost 60 percent of the patients were there at the
insistence of their employers. It appears that we have a way
to go in this country toward developing this type of attitude
in employer-employee relations.

Finally, the usefulness of this warning sign appears to be
of minimal significance percentage-wise because of the great
importance attached to having a job. The fact that a given
patient has never been fired or warned is used by their
spouses or themselves as an indication that they have no
problem with alcohol. It reflects a priority system that holds
that one can lose one's family, money, or freedom (through
arrest) but the job is the last to go. In fact, those first-time
patients who are seeking treatment because of the loss of a
job or a warning about their performance are usually well on
their way to crossing the line if they haven't crossed already.

9. Medically-related problems.

A series of medically-related problems provides warning
signs to the professional staff that alcohol is taking its toll on
the body organs and on health in general. At least 80 percent
of our patients admitted for the first time, when asked the
question "How is your health in general?" will answer
positively "Pretty good." Fortunately, from a preventative
medical point of view, nine times out of ten they are

essentially correct. It is my perception that people with an alcohol problem are seeking treatment earlier in the disease process, thereby providing the opportunity to deflect them from a self-destructive pathway. I hasten to add that we do see many patients who are severely physically and emotionally ill secondary to the complications of alcoholism. But in general, these more severe cases tend to be patients who have relapsed and are being readmitted for the second or third time, rather than the younger persons being admitted for the first time.

a. Major Medical Problems.   The major medical complications we see, in descending order of prevalence, include: acute alcoholic hepatitis (damage to the liver), major depression (a psychiatric disorder), chronic obstructive pulmonary disease (damage to the lungs), alcoholic cardiomyopathy (damage to the heart), and macrocytosis (a disturbance in red blood cell production due to a nutritional deficiency). More will be said about these problems when we discuss the medical complications of alcoholism.

b. Hypertension, Ulcers, and Liver Damage.   The two most frequent medical problems described by our patients who were diagnosed and treated by their private physicians are high blood pressure (hypertension), and ulcers (peptic ulcer disease). Approximately 60 percent of the patients seen in Ignatia Hall have an elevated blood pressure at the time of admission and many bring along their blood pressure medications. The majority of these patients eventually confess that they have never told their doctors about their alcohol problem. In most instances, we discontinue these medicines for the first three to four days to determine the degree of influence of alcohol on their blood pressure. About 80 percent of these patients with elevated blood pressures at the time of admission will be discharged eight days later with a normal blood pressure and no pills. The other 20 percent will have to be started on their medicines again, because their high blood pressure does not appear to be related to alcohol intake. The close relationship between alcohol intake and blood pressure deserves closer attention on the part of physicians, especially because of the direct relationship shown between high alcohol intake and stroke.

A very high percentage of our patients (80 to 90 percent) complain of an upset stomach, or an acid taste in their mouths, or a burning in their stomachs soon after admission. Experience shows that the majority of these patients have an acute gastritis that will heal with Maalox (antacids), regular meals, and, of course, no alcohol. About 10 percent of these patients will have persistent pain or discomfort and eventually prove to have a peptic ulcer, as revealed by an upper G.I. (gastrointestinal) X-ray series. Appropriate ulcer treatment will then be started.

A significant number of patients, usually those who have had previous alcoholism treatment, will state that their doctors told them they had cirrhosis of the liver and had better stop drinking. Further probing, however, reveals that no thorough diagnostic work-up was carried out to validate a diagnosis of cirrhosis. The usual procedure should include a needle biopsy of the liver, a process most would be very likely to remember. It appears that in many of these cases, the patient had an acute alcoholic hepatitis, but cirrhosis of the liver is better known and more feared by the general public. Although this approach of using the "big stick" and scaring the patient into stopping drinking can be successful, it can also backfire. I have seen patients who have taken the position that "If I'm going to die, I might as well keep right on drinking." Again, more on this topic when we return to the medical complications of alcoholism.

c. Trauma. When taking medical histories, we ask patients "Have you ever had any broken bones, serious cuts, lacerations, or a concussion?" If the answers are in the affirmative, we then ask when and how it happened, and whether alcohol was misused at the time. About 40 percent of our patients have had a bone fracture related to alcohol, such as falling down or being involved in a fight while drunk. The age at which the event took place varies, but in general the majority occurred within five years of admission. Nearly half of the patients who experienced some type of broken bone(s) say it happened in a car accident when either the patient or some other person was driving drunk. About 5 percent broke one or more bones when involved in a motorcycle accident while drinking. Again, any type of injury that is alcohol related should be noted as a warning sign.

d. Minor Medical Problems. The most common minor medical signs and symptoms our patients associate with drinking are heart palpitations ("My heart feels like it's going to jump out of my chest"), loss of appetite ("When I drink, I don't eat"), nausea with morning vomiting or the dry heaves, abdominal pain ("It feels like my stomach is in knots") and diarrhea ("Loose, watery stool when I'm drinking").

e. Numbness and Tingling of Hands and Feet.   This symptom of numbness and tingling of the fingers and toes—"My feet are always going to sleep"—deserves special attention because it relates to the development of what is called peripheral neuropathy, or damage to sensory nerves of the arms and legs. This is an important symptom to be aware of, because corrective steps can be taken after one stops drinking. The peripheral neuropathy, in most cases, is due to one aspect of malnutrition that often accompanies drinking, namely, the development of a vitamin B_1 (thiamine) deficiency. This deficiency can be corrected, depending on the severity of damage to the nerves in the extremities. Usually, nerve function can be restored by including extra vitamin B_1 in the diet. Our usual practice is to have vitamin-deficient patients take a 100mg tablet twice a day for two months or so, depending on the degree of damage to the nerves. More about this later.

f. Leg Cramps or Charley Horses.   A significant number of our patients report severe, if not excruciatingly painful, leg cramps, usually at night when they are in bed. By the second or third day of abstaining from drinking, the severity and frequency diminish. By the fifth day, the problem is usually no longer present. The cause of the night cramps is not completely understood. Some have suggested that it is due to a toxic effect of alcohol or acetaldehyde causing the destruction of the muscle cells called sarcolysis. Others feel it is due to a disruption of the body's chemistry in the form of excessive lactic acid production, or possibly it's a disturbance in salt or mineral metabolism, particularly sodium and potassium. The result is a stabbing pain that makes grown men cry when they get these cramps.

10. Sexual Problems.

In response to the question "What happens to your interest in sexual activity when you are drinking?" men and women over the age of thirty, in general, described a decreased interest in sex. "When I drink, the last thing I think about is sex," is not an uncommon remark from this group. On the other hand, men and women under age thirty, in general, will describe an increased interest in sex when drinking—"I'm less inhibited" or "I seem to get more sexy when I'm drinking." The entire matter of the effects of alcohol on sexual activity and responses is really too complex to be discussed in this short book.

Many of our patients fifty years and older will describe how they haven't slept in the same bed as their spouse for years because of "my drinking problem." Others will talk about how their interest in sex has been going steadily downhill, which they attribute to getting older and don't believe is even remotely related to their drinking problem. Women in their third decade of life and older tend to just shrug their shoulders when asked about sexual activity and interest, as if it were the lowest priority on a scale of life's activities. It should be emphasized that a high percentage of women patients in our unit are emotionally depressed when they are admitted. A relatively few male patients in their thirties, forties, and fifties will complain of impotency (inability to gain an erection), but many will complain about being unable to "perform like I used to when I was younger." In general, we can conclude that those whose consumption of alcohol is bringing them closer to the line have a decreased libido or have no interest in sexual activity.

11. Emotional Problems and Depression.

Approximately 35 percent of our patients have had previous hospitalizations in a psychiatric unit or have seen a psychiatrist or a psychologist on an out-patient basis. This statistic may be misleading, however, because in many communities, detoxification from alcohol may routinely take place in psychiatric units rather than specialized alcohol treatment centers. Also, some of this 35 percent of patients were admitted to psychiatric units because of abnormal or inappropriate behavior due to the acute effects of intoxication. These types of psychiatric admissions are usually short term—two to three days—in order for the person to sober up. More than half of the patients who report a previous psychiatric admission list depression as the reason.

When we ask patients being admitted to our center how they are feeling, ("Are you down, or high, or stable?") about 90 percent report that they are feeling down or depressed. Part of their depression can be related to feelings of embarrassment, fear, guilt, and just plain old feeling sick. After several days in our center, their emotions and mental status start to improve. However, the features of depression persist to a significant degree in about one-fourth of the patients, whom our psychiatrist is asked to see. In general, the diagnosis in most of these cases is a major depressive disorder. However, the difficulty is in determining whether depression is the primary disorder—that is, that it predates the alcohol problem—or a secondary disorder related to the effects of alcohol. Since different forms of therapy are called for in treating primary versus secondary types of depression, this can be a very troublesome problem in designing a treatment program. I will talk about the problem of dual diagnosis or dual disease more later, but clearly some individuals have two diseases at the same time—some form of mental illness plus alcoholism.

12. Genetic Factors.

In the course of obtaining the pertinent medical and psychosocial history from each patient, by which the previous warning signs have been documented, I have found that by the time I get to asking questions about family history—did your mother or father ever have a drinking problem?—I can predict that nine out of ten times the answer will be yes. For the one patient out of ten who answers no, a further question regarding grandparents, uncles, or aunts, either paternal or maternal, will bring a yes answer. Because the role of genetic factors is so important, a separate chapter will be devoted to this topic.

Summary of Warning Signs

For your convenience and review, here are the warning signs just described:

1. Cigarette smoking and nicotine dependence
2. Blackouts
3. Attendance at AA meetings prior to first alcoholism treatment
4. Attempts to stop drinking
5. Use of illicit drugs or abuse of prescription drugs
6. Arrests for alcohol-related offenses
7. Multiple divorces associated with drinking problem
8. Fired or warned on the job

9. Medically related problems:
   a. Major medical problems
   b. Diagnosis and treatment of hypertension, peptic ulcers, or liver damage
   c. Trauma
   d. Minor medical problems:
      1. loss of appetite
      2. nausea and morning vomiting or dry heaves
      3. stomach pain and cramps
      4. diarrhea
   e. Numbness and tingling of hands and feet
   f. Leg cramps or charley horses
10. Sexual problems
11. Emotional problems and depression
12. Genetic factors

This is not a checklist to make a diagnosis of the disease of alcoholism. There are a variety of self-tests and diagnostic tests available through Alcoholics Anonymous and other groups. This list summarizes the physical, emotional, and social changes that our patients tell us about in their medical histories when they are admitted to our treatment program. Since at least 80 to 85 percent of our patients go through the signs and symptoms of withdrawal when they enter the program, we feel it's safe to say that any person who drinks alcohol and experiences any of these social and physical changes should take heed: they may be in the process of crossing the line. When does one cross the line? When does a cucumber become a pickle? But remember, also, that a pickle can never become a cucumber again.

The most important message I can give is that it may still

be possible to turn back. I am frequently asked, "How many of these warning signs must be present before I start worrying?" My answer is, "The presence of only one may be significant when it is linked to alcohol." Again, let me emphasize that we are talking about potential predictors and that this list will probably get longer as we continue to learn more about the disease.

FIVE

Genetic Factors and Alcoholism

We pay a great deal of attention to the presence or absence of alcoholism in a patient's family. First, it provides added information in arriving at the diagnosis of alcoholism in a particular person. It also reinforces the idea of the inheritability of the disease and provides an incentive to focus on preventing development of the disease in those members of the family who may be susceptible.

Let me tell you about Tim. He was twenty-two years old when he was admitted to our center with a diagnosis of alcoholism. While his history was taken, he stated that neither his father, his mother, or his two brothers had a drinking problem. "I'm the only black sheep in the family," he said.

During the first week, Tim was very quiet, never smiled, and stayed off by himself. When I arrived in the unit on Saturday morning to do rounds, Tim was waiting at the elevator, all smiles, and greeted me enthusiastically. The transformation in his behavior was almost like a miracle.

Upon questioning Tim, I learned that his mother had come to the open AA meeting on Friday night at St. Thomas Hospital (this AA meeting has been held every Friday night for almost fifty years). After the meeting, Tim's mother walked with him to the elevator as he prepared to return to the center. Tim then described how he had hugged and kissed his mother good night (something he hadn't done in years) when his mother unexpectedly said that she was going up to the unit with him. "No, Mom," Tim said, "You can't come up unless you are a patient or a recovering alcoholic." Tim described the next event with tears in his eyes. His mother said, "There is something I never told you, but twenty-three years ago, the year before you were born, I was a patient at Ignatia Hall."

I suspect everyone might act a little different upon hearing something like that for the first time, but to Tim it was apparently a great moment, for he said to me, "Doc, I'm not the only black sheep in the family."

It has long been common knowledge that alcoholism runs in families. However, only in recent years, with major advances in the field of genetics, has the full impact of this message been appreciated. When asked, "To the best of your knowledge, has your father ever had an alcohol problem?" the answer, for more than 50 percent of both male and female patients is affirmative:

"Yes, Dad's an alcoholic."

"Dad used to drink, but he has been sober for years."

"I don't remember my dad, he died when I was little, but Mom says he had a drinking problem."

"Yes, Dad died of cirrhosis of the liver because he was an alcoholic."

"Yeah, Dad was a drunk!"

The "like father, like son" analogy does not permit one to conclude whether the similarity is due to genetic factors, or what are referred to as environmental factors—Dad serving as a role model. Approximately 25 percent of both male and female patients describe their mother as being an alcoholic. To date we have identified 300 patients out of more than six thousand who describe both parents as alcoholics.

I had a nineteen-year-old patient who gave me the following family history: "When I was six years old, my father and uncle would take me with them to hit all the bars on East Market Street several times a week, and many times we would all come home drunk." This young man entered his first alcoholism treatment program at the age of ten. He came from an ethnic group that held you were not a man unless you could "hold your liquor." At the age of sixteen he entered another program, and at the age of nineteen, when I met him, he was in the surgery intensive care unit recovering from multiple fractures received in an auto accident during a blackout. Both his father and his uncle died of complications of alcoholism. One would have little trouble concluding that alcoholism runs in *this* family, but did the young man inherit a drinking problem, or did he learn it from East Market Street—his environment? It is not possible to know. When I ask incoming patients when they tasted alcohol for the first time, I get a lot of answers like: "Hey, I'm Italian. There was wine on the table ever since I can remember."

Going through fifty years of records kept by Ignatia Hall, we have identified at least thirty families in which the grandfather, the son, and the grandson had all been patients in our treatment facility. In fact, since we began an extended care program (twenty-one days) in addition to our acute care program (eight days in duration) there have been three or four instances where a father has been in one unit and his son in the other. Yet in spite of observing the disease in three generations of at least thirty different families, this could still reflect the influence of an environmental background ("If Grandad and Dad can drink, then I can drink") rather than a genetic factor.

However, convincing evidence of the role of the genes on the development of alcoholism is beginning to emerge. To date, the best evidence has appeared in what are generally called the adoption studies. These studies, conducted primarily in Scandinavia, reviewed the family history of individuals treated for alcoholism. An oversimplified summary of the results indicates that if identical twins of parents who were alcoholic (either parent, or both, but particularly the father) were placed in separate foster homes before three years of age—whether these homes were drinking homes or nondrinking—the probability of both adopted children developing alcoholism was very high. Control studies that included identical twins from nonalcoholic parents placed in separate foster homes (drinking and nondrinking) had a very low probability of developing alcoholism, even if raised in a drinking environment. These studies are being expanded and made more sophisticated, including measurement of levels of the acetaldehyde and other alcohol breakdown products in the blood. The tests seek to find any differences between the blood levels of the alcoholic patient after receiving a standard dose of alcohol, and nonalcoholic siblings and other family members. The forthcoming results of such research may eventually permit us to predict which children are genetically susceptible to develop the disease as they grow up. Better still, these types of studies may someday provide an answer to the question, "What causes alcoholism?"

Experimental animal studies carried out for several years have demonstrated that certain genetic strains of mice, rats and hamsters, given a choice between plain drinking water and water containing between 5 and 10 percent alcohol, will prefer the alcohol over the water.

This preference for alcohol has been shown to be genetically determined, since animals (dogs, cats, and other household pets) in general have an aversion to alcohol.

Researchers are now trying to find a way to determine whether this preference for alcohol is due to a genetically determined taste or a genetically determined activity of the brain's chemistry, possibly similar to the compulsive drinking discussed earlier in this book.

While the final word on the role of genetics in alcoholism is far from in, the evidence for a genetic factor(s) is becoming increasingly convincing. How does this influence the treatment of the disease, and how do patients react to the implication that their disease was inherited? Frankly, some, like Tim, are relieved—"I don't have to feel guilty?" or "I'm not really a bad person?"—while others are angry: "Why did this have to happen to me?"

I tell my patients that I have a genetically determined disease myself: a lactose intolerance, which means I cannot drink milk or eat most milk products. If I drink a glass of milk, after thirty to forty-five minutes I develop severe diarrhea, intestinal gas, and cramping. Up until the age of forty-one, I loved milk and ice cream, but then the problem started. My mother developed the same disease when she was in her early forties, and my sister developed the problem at the same age. But neither my father nor my brother have had any problems with milk. I recall rather vividly how the rest of the family began to question whether Mom was having some psychosomatic problems. After all, at that time it was considered almost un-American not to drink milk. Today we know that the concentration of a specific enzyme (lactase) decreases with age in certain individuals. The major sugar in milk is lactose. When we drink a glass of milk, our intestinal lining, where this enzyme is located, cannot break down the lactose sugar properly. This creates a metabolic imbalance which brings about a disturbance in the gastrointestinal system, including diarrhea, trapped gas, and cramping. In effect, what we have is a genetically determined disease that is progressive, meaning that it becomes worse with age. The treatment? No milk! As long as I stay away from milk, milk shakes, ice cream, and certain creamed soups, I feel fine. I must confess there are times when I slip, either forgetting or willing to risk it—"a little bit won't hurt me." Let me assure you, I can't fool my body, and thirty to forty minutes later I pay the consequences.

Looking at alcoholism in the same manner, we believe it is a genetically determined disease that is progressive, and the signs and symptoms can be avoided or controlled by consuming no alcohol! Some patients become upset over the fate of their children when they learn that this disease can be inherited. An explanation, though oversimplified, appears to reassure them:

"Let's assume I am genetically susceptible to developing cancer, and you are not. We both go to some deserted island where there are no cancer-causing agents like certain viruses, tobacco smoke, or chemical pollutants in the air. Neither one of us will develop cancer. But then we both move to a city with a significant level of pollutants in the air that have been shown to produce cancer at least in experimental animals. I will develop cancer and you will not, in spite of us both being exposed to the same environment. The same is true of cigarette smokers; some will develop heart and lung disease and others will not, depending on their genetic susceptibility. It is also a practical explanation of why a person sitting on your left at a bar and another sitting on your right can drink without any apparent long-term effects, and you, the alcoholic, cannot drink."

Supposing you or your spouse, or perhaps both of you, have been diagnosed as alcoholics: your children are very susceptible to developing the disease. What can you do to prevent it from developing in them? Educate them; tell them honestly and plainly that they are very likely to be genetically susceptible to becoming an alcoholic, like you or your spouse, including all the misery and complications you know well. However, the disease can only be prevented if they follow one rule: "Don't Drink." Remember, you must drink alcohol to develop the signs and symptoms of alcoholism.

SIX

Medical Complications of Alcohol

Alcohol can damage any and every organ of the body with the possible exception of the kidney. Because the majority of patients seen in our center have become physically dependent on alcohol—have crossed the line—it was hard not to link physical dependency and medical complications when they were detected. We made the assumption that first one became physically dependent on alcohol, and that medical complications came later. This has proved to be a wrong assumption.

Years ago, Ohio passed a law that required anyone who had been ticketed for a second DWI (driving while intoxicated) or DUI (driving under the influence) to choose between ten days in jail or ten days in an alcohol treatment program. Soon the courts were referring patients to Ignatia Hall, and patients were presenting themselves for treatment on the advice of their lawyers. These court-ordered patients proved to be most interesting from a medical and statistical point of view. We were able to see a broad cross section of potential alcoholics earlier in the progression of the disease than our usual admissions, 80 percent of whom had crossed the line.

In most instances, upon admission this court-ordered group gave a history of no alcohol intake for periods of several days, weeks, or even months, depending on their trial date and other factors. They also showed signs of anger, embarrassment, and frustration and definitely insisted they did not have a drinking problem: "I just happened to be at the wrong place at the wrong time!" These patients were treated like any others admitted to the center for their first alcohol treatment. I was not surprised to find that the majority of these patients had relatively few medical problems. The problems we found were conditions similar to what you might expect to find in a so-called normal group of people of similar ages including stuffed-up noses, aching joints and muscles, and, if smokers, a chronic cough. However, about thirty to forty percent of these patients reported that they had experienced blackouts, were having marital problems related to their drinking, had been warned at work about absenteeism and, of course, had at least two or more drinking and driving citations—many of the warning signs described earlier.

Surprisingly a very significant percentage of this court-ordered group also showed evidence of liver injury, as revealed by laboratory tests, or had a history of hypertension: "My doctor had trouble prescribing the right medicine and kept telling me to cut down on salt, lose weight, and cut down on alcohol," or "Yes, I have had numbness in my hands and feet in the past." Many of this group also had a history of peptic ulcers, pancreatitis, or psychiatric treatment—mainly for depression. Many also reported a loss of interest in sex:

"I can't perform like I used to." In others, laboratory tests showed enlarged red blood cells, a sign of poor nutrition. The point to be made is that alcohol can be damaging the body organs before the phase of physical dependency is reached. It can cause damage in the recreational drinker, the psychologically dependent drinker, and even earlier in the course of the disease. Indeed, as described earlier, the toxic effects of alcohol consumption can occur even in those not addicted to alcohol, depending on the amount and duration of drinking. In short, you do not have to be an alcoholic to cause damage to your body. I'm certain this early damage is not a new idea to many of my colleagues, and this is no claim for a new discovery. However, it was an important revelation to me, and I share it as part of my attempt to understand this complicated disease.

I repeat: "Alcohol can affect every organ of the body." The liver, as mentioned earlier, is extremely vulnerable to injury. There are a host of so-called minor ills as well:

• Skin rashes can appear or be worsened by heavy drinking, including psoriasis and different kinds of eczema. Sometimes we see an intensification of acne over the face and back.

• All three pairs of salivary glands increase in size in many alcoholic patients, with acute episodes of swelling of the parotid gland just in front of the jaw. It almost mimics the mumps. Some patients have scarring of the esophagus to the degree that they can't swallow solid foods.

• A significant number of our patients complain of a sharp, localized pain in their stomach region that proves to be a peptic ulcer on the X-rays. Some complain of a similar type of pain, but add that the pain seems to radiate straight through their body as if someone were ramming a hot poker through them—which is a classic description of injury to the pancreas, or pancreatitis.

• Some patients describe bright red blood in the stool, and a rectal examination usually supports a diagnosis of hemorrhoids rather than cancer of the colon. The hemorrhoids become a greater problem when the patient is experiencing a great deal of diarrhea secondary to heavy drinking.

• As mentioned earlier, some of our patients complain of night cramps or charley horses when engaged in heavy drinking. Laboratory tests reveal the presence of significant injury to the muscle cells. Usually, the night cramps go away by the second or third day of admission when the patient starts eating again and has had no alcohol.

• Nearly half of the patients admitted to our center will have a borderline or abnormal electrocardiogram (EKG). The most frequent abnormality is cardiac arrhythmia, or irregular heartbeats. In the majority of these patients, the electrocardiogram returns to normal in three to four days after admission. However, in about 10 percent of the patients, the abnormal EKG can be attributed to the alcoholic cardiac myopathy, or permanent damage to the heart walls.

• "Doc, my big toe is killing me!" A physical exam will usually reveal redness, swelling, and tenderness of the big toe. Lab tests will show an elevated blood uric acid level. All it takes is observing uric acid crystals under the microscope in the sample of fluid taken from the big toe joint to diagnose a case of gout. We find a high uric acid level in more than 50 percent of our patients when they are first admitted, which is best correlated to a high blood alcohol level. Not every patient with a high uric acid level develops gout. In 95 percent of these patients, the blood uric acid level returns to normal within three to four days. Our experience would suggest that a significant number of people being treated by their family physicians for gout are presenting a symptom of heavy drinking. Unfortunately, they are being treated for a symptom, not the disease!

• Because almost all of our patients smoke cigarettes, there are frequent complaints of difficulty in breathing and of coughing up various amounts of phlegm, ranging from clear to grayish-brown, particularly in the morning after arising. Interestingly, they generally will deny ever coughing up any blood. Of course, with the prevalence of smoking history, many of our patients have developed a chronic obstructive pulmonary disease (COPD), or, as they know it, emphysema.

• Although enlargement of the male breasts (called gyne-comastia) and atrophy or shrinking of the testes are talked about in medical textbooks, I have seen fewer than five patients out of more than five thousand with either or both of these findings. On the other hand, I have seen at least a dozen young men between the ages of twenty-five and thirty, who gave a history of smoking at least five reefers or joints of marijuana daily for several years, who had quite striking enlargements of their breasts due to an increase in the glandular portion of the breasts, and not to fat tissue.

• Another observation is a seemingly high number of patients with excessive wax (cerumen) buildup in their ears. In some patients this wax is literally "hard as a rock," and it takes ear drops to soften it over a three-day period before it is flushed out by irrigating with warm water. It always pleases me when one of the patients exclaims after this treatment, "My God, I can hear again; I thought I was going deaf!"

• Another impressive finding is the increased frequency of dental caries and the number of twenty- to thirty-year-old men with dentures. We could speculate that the poor dental status is due to a combination of factors, including socioeconomic, nutritional, lifestyle, and alcohol.

As this list indicates, nearly every organ and system of the body is affected by alcohol except possibly the kidney. We often see signs of what appears to be an infection of the lower urinary tract (bladder and urethra) as well as the presence of red blood cells in the urine (microhematuria), but laboratory studies do not reveal the presence of bacteria. Three or four days later, when the urine test is repeated, the results will usually be normal. We have tentatively decided that this finding might be due to the irritating and dehydrating effects of alcohol on the lining of the bladder and urethra. After all, approximately 5 percent of the alcohol consumed is excreted in the urine. High blood alcohol levels for long periods of time from heavy drinking could seemingly produce a very toxic urine.

As for the kidney, a colleague who is a kidney specialist (nephrologist) commented recently that he had never seen our alcoholism treatment center. It suddenly occurred to me that over the past five years, I have asked for consultations from just about every medical and surgical specialist in St. Thomas Medical Center, but I had yet to ask for a consult from a nephrologist. Our patients do not seem to develop kidney problems.

One laboratory finding may eventually provide solid ground

for diagnosing alcoholism from a blood sample. The majority of our patients *are not anemic* at the time of admission, although we might well suspect anemia because of the reported suppression of the bone marrow by alcohol. We do see the occasional male patient with hemoglobin levels of 10 to 11 grams percent (normal for the male is about 14 grams percent), and various blood tests support the finding that the anemia is alcohol related. However, we do see a significant number of patients who have normal *numbers* of red blood cells, and, in turn, normal levels of hemoglobin, but the *size* of the red blood cells is abnormal. A laboratory measurement called the mean corpuscular volume (MCV) indicates the relative size of the red blood cells in the patient. The normal range of values for men is 83 to 95mm^3 (cubic millimeters), and, for women, 81 to 93mm^3. I have been impressed with the number of male patients with values over 100mm^3. The highest we have seen to date in a man was 130mm^3. The highest MCV we have measured in a woman patient was 120mm^3. What this means in simple terms is that these patients have *larger* red blood cells than normal people. What effect does this have on your health? As far as we know today, none, except that it means your body is not functioning at its top efficiency. What causes the increased size in red blood cells?

The presence of the large red blood cells is a red flag indicating that the patient is probably showing signs of deficiency of an important vitaminlike chemical called *folic acid*. In effect, the patient is suffering from malnutrition. This could be caused either by not eating regularly, or because the heavy intake of alcohol blocks the absorption of water-soluble vitamins and other nutrients, including folic acid, from the intestinal tract. However, our recent studies suggest that the presence of large red blood cells is more likely caused by a direct effect of alcohol on the bone marrow, which is producing the red blood cells. We have found that it takes as long as four months after one stops drinking for the size of the circulating red blood cells to return to normal. This relates to the 120-day life span of the human red blood cell. Basically, all the injured red blood cells must die off; then new ones that have not been exposed to alcohol appear.

Can one who is an impulsive drinker, or even a social drinker, as described earlier, ignore the possibility of developing medical complications? How much is too much? More specifically, is any person who drinks alcoholic beverages at risk to develop medical complications?

What may be a harmless amount of alcohol for one person may well be potentially damaging to another. Obviously, a person who doesn't drink any alcoholic beverages is not at risk of developing alcohol-related damage to body organs, but a minimum safe level of alcohol intake has not been determined. Just as scientists have been struggling to determine the minimum safe level of radiation, tobacco smoke, or exposure to a variety of toxic pollutants, it is difficult to say what is a minimum safe level of alcohol intake.

"But, Doctor, how can I find out whether I'm drinking too much so that it is hurting my body?" some ask. My answer is, in part, to check with his or her physician and make sure he or she does a battery of liver function tests that measure different enzymes or secretions of the liver in the blood. Any injury or damage to the liver will show up as an increase in the blood level of these enzymes, because they will leak out into the blood stream when there is liver cell injury. The higher the blood level of the enzymes, the greater the damage to the liver. The good news is that these values, in most cases, will return to normal levels after one stops drinking or at least cuts down on the alcohol intake, because, as mentioned earlier, the liver has a tremendous capacity to regenerate or heal itself.

Cholesterol, diet, and heart disease are receiving a great deal of attention, and most people ask their doctors to include a blood cholesterol determination in a battery of lab tests. Alcohol can cause an elevated cholesterol level, but this will usually return to lower values when you stop drinking. About 40 percent of our patients will have a high cholesterol level (greater than 200mg%) when first admitted to our center, but 90 percent of these patients will be discharged one to three weeks later with a normal level (below 200mg%). Whether this alcohol-induced elevation of blood cholesterol plays a role in the increased incidence of heart disease in alcoholics remains to be determined. The recent evidence that moderate drinking (two drinks a day or less) may actually protect a person from developing heart disease has supported the old saying "A glass or two of wine a day is good for you." But any public health recommendation to encourage moderate drinking in view of the toll exacted by alcohol in terms of hospitalizations, useful life years lost, and mortality would be very dangerous.

One may also ask his physician to do a complete blood count (CBC) including the mean corpuscular volume (MCV) of the red blood cells. These tests, along with an overall physical examination, will show some of the earliest signs of changes or injury to the body due to alcohol. I also suggest this should be done once a year.

Some may argue that if one is that concerned, it would be much simpler just not to drink. But despite the potential problems, many people will continue to drink as routinely as they eat. Both food and alcohol are always around us.

Alcohol and the Nervous System

Alcohol can and does damage the brain and the rest of the nervous system. This damage can occur through at least two mechanisms: one is the direct effect of alcohol or its breakdown product (acetaldehyde). The other is an indirect mechanism acting upon the lining of the intestinal tract, which blocks the absorption of water-soluble nutrients in the diet, particularly B_1 or thiamine.

If I have heard a patient say it once, I must have heard it a thousand times: "Doc, I drink, but I eat three meals a day." Somehow it has become widely accepted that as long as one eats regularly, he or she will be protected from the damaging effects of alcohol. The reality is that if one is drinking too much for his or her particular body makeup, all the water-soluble nutrients in the diet will enter one orifice (the mouth) and leave by way of another orifice (the anus). Relatively little of these nutrients will be absorbed into the circulation and distributed throughout the body due to the blockage of the intestinal lining by the alcohol being consumed. One patient who confronted me on this topic said, "Doc, I drank every day, but I took multivitamins every morning." My response was, "You might as well have given the money you spent on the vitamins to your favorite charity for all the good they are doing you." Again, the dilemma is how much is too much.

It is estimated that a person can develop a vitamin B_1 or thiamine deficiency in as little as seven to ten days, especially when drinking heavily and eating poorly. Actually, we just assume that every patient admitted to our center, as mentioned earlier, is suffering from malnutrition. Our standing medical orders include injecting 100mg (milligrams) of vitamin B_1 each day for the first four days. Many patients don't relish the thought of getting the shots. When they ask why they can't take it by mouth, we explain that their drinking prior to admission probably affects the lining of the intestines for several days following the last drink. If we gave the vitamin by mouth during this period, it would probably pass right through with no benefit to the body.

What are the symptoms of B_1 deficiency in the brain and nervous system? The most common symptom we hear about is numbness and tingling (paraesthesias) in the hands and feet. This is called peripheral neuropathy. The condition is more or less severe depending on the duration of the drinking, the amounts consumed, nutritional status, and, of course, age.

One extreme example of neuropathy related to drinking is worth telling. The patient was a sixty-four-year-old retired telephone operator who lived alone in a third-floor apartment of a three-story building that had a tavern at street level. She had a severe alcoholism problem, including physical dependency, and had reached a point where the neuropathy prevented her from walking; she could only crawl around her apartment. Fearful of the shakes and tremors of withdrawal, she visited the tavern downstairs daily. Unable to walk, she would take a pillow and slide down the stairs, then wait until some kind soul picked her up and carried her into the tavern. After she consumed seven or eight bottles of beer and a few mixed drinks, another kind soul would carry her up to her apartment. This was her daily existence for several months. Food, of course, was the farthest thing from her mind.

One day her son, who lived out of town, came to see her. He was shocked to find her, by then, unable even to crawl and took her to the hospital. There was much discussion at the hospital about whether she should be admitted to our treatment center, because of her severe medical/neurological problems. The son insisted that she should be admitted to Ignatia Hall because her basic problem was alcoholism. We agreed with him on that point, but tried to explain that we were not geared to take patients with such severe medical problems because they had to walk to the various activities. For whatever reason, probably a combination of feeling sorry for the woman and the realization that she had to be treated for alcoholism before she destroyed herself, we admitted her to our center. With tender loving nursing care, feeding her, bathing her, good nutrition and rest, injections of vitamin B_1 for the first few days, and then by mouth for the next fourteen days, and, of course, no alcohol, the patient actually walked out of the center under her own power on the day of discharge with only the aid of a walker device. In addition to this striking physical improvement, she showed increasing interest and involvement in the various activities of group therapy, movies, lectures, and AA meetings. The latest report from the son, with whom she is now living, is that "Mom is doing great!"

There is a whole range of clinical conditions that reflect damage to the brain associated with alcoholism, and entire books have been written about them. To serve our purposes, let me cite three cases:

CASE 1

Ralph, a forty-four-year-old patient, was very intoxicated when he presented himself to our admitting desk. Feeling little or no pain, he was joking with our staff during the admission interview. I happened to be passing by, and he grabbed my arm and managed to tell me, in slurred speech, "Doc, the reason I drink is because I was a helicopter pilot in Vietnam, and every time I get flashbacks about strafing villages with women and children, I feel so terrible I get drunk." After reassuring him that we would take care of this later, I mentally stored the information.

Ralph had a rough withdrawal experience, and on Day Seven he was still staggering down the hallway with what is called a widegait stagger. We did a CAT scan of his brain, and the diagnosis was cerebral and cerebellar atrophy—moderate, which, in simple terms, is a shriveling-up of the brain. We started him on high doses of vitamin B_1 by mouth; he was eating well, and, of course, drinking no alcohol. By Day Twelve he was walking more normally. At this time I decided to talk to him about his "guilt feelings" and traumatic experiences in Vietnam. I started off with something like: "Ralph, do you want to talk about Vietnam?" He gave me a puzzled look, which deepened when I followed this with, "You know, when you were a helicopter pilot?" Still bewildered, he finally declared, "Doc, I've never been out of Ohio!"

CASE 2

Jerry was a massive man, about 6 feet, five inches tall and weighing 275 pounds. I was alone with him in our examining room soon after he was admitted, asking about his psychosocial and medical history, when all of a sudden he reached across the table, grabbed my wrist, and squeezed it so tightly I thought he would crush every bone in my hand. Then he looked at me straight in the eye and asked, "Doc, do you know why I'm here?"

Still totally surprised, I managed to get out, "Why, to deal with your alcohol problem."

"No, no, no, I'm here because I just killed the warden and six guards at Lucasville [state prison]." Needless to say, many thoughts were racing through my mind, not the least of which was, "How am I going to get out of here?" To make a long story short, four or five days later Jerry was telling us how he had never been away from his farm, which was in a nearby community, in his entire life. The warden and guards at Lucasville appeared to be alive and well. And his wife and other family members confirmed that he had never served a prison term.

CASE 3

Joe was a sixty-five-year-old truck driver who had been on a disability pension for ten years and had about eight years of sobriety when he relapsed. After about three months of progressively heavier drinking, he had been drinking almost around the clock for five or six days when his daughter brought him to the center. She said he had been acting strangely lately and apparently believed he was still married to the wife he had divorced five years earlier.

During the admission history and physical, we found a severely scarred left upper arm with some bony disfigurements. When I asked how the arm had been injured, I heard a most interesting war story. (As a veteran of World War II, war stories have a special interest for me.) Joe's story was that he had served in the U.S. Marines and was engaged in a mopping up operation on the island of Guam shortly after the peace treaty was signed. He was leaning against the trunk of a coconut tree when suddenly a rifle fell from the top of the tree and smashed against his upper left arm. The rifle belonged to a Japanese soldier hiding in the top of the tree. Joe remarked, "I'm sure lucky that Japanese soldier didn't have any bullets left." The surgeon at the field hospital felt the injured arm required more specialized treatment, and Joe was flown back to the States. Soon after he was discharged from the Marine Corps, he started working for a trucking firm until his disability pension for emphysema was approved twenty years later. On the tenth day of this hospitalization, Joe complained that his left arm was beginning to be very painful, and I decided to have an orthopedist come in to consult. Whatever possessed me to ask him again how he had injured his arm I don't know, but I was almost sorry I did, because it ruined a good war story. Joe's answer this time was, "It was that darned country doctor's fault; he didn't know what he was doing." I supposed the Navy could have had some former country doctors serving in the Pacific war zone, and I thought nothing of it until he continued with, "I fell out of my grandma's apple tree when I was three years old [pointing to the disfigured left arm] and the country doctor down the road really didn't know what to do with it." As the true story unfolded, Joe was rejected for

military service because of the disfigured arm which occurred when he was three years old.

These three cases are examples of a clinical condition associated
with injury to the brain observed in alcoholic patients which
is referred to as *confabulation*, that is, living out fantasies. In
many instances, a good nutritious diet, rest, no alcohol, and
daily administration of vitamin B_1 can bring about a striking
recovery of brain functions and, in turn, normalization of
behavior.

One of the challenges in treating a patient who shows
signs of abnormal brain function is to determine whether
this is alcohol-related, or some other disease process is
taking place. For some as yet unknown reason, we have been
seeing an increasing number of patients over sixty-five years
old who are presenting themselves for treatment for the first
time in their lives. The oldest male patient to date was
eighty-nine years old, and the oldest female patient was
eighty-eight. We are currently studying this phenomenon,
and it raises such questions as whether there might be a
late-onset type of alcoholism. When older patients act con-
fused or have inappropriate behavior, it is a challenge for the
staff to figure out whether we are dealing with the effects of
alcohol, or what is called an organic brain syndrome due to
hardening of the brain's blood vessels. Let me tell you about
Carl, a seventy-six-year-old retired movie house operator
who had left Ohio to retire in the South.

Carl was beginning to have trouble remembering things
and began to be careless in his dress and personal hygiene.
His daughter insisted that he come back home and live with
her and her family for a while. This didn't work out, but,

concerned for his well-being, she encouraged him to take up residence in a local senior citizens' home. One day he was found drunk in his room. The physician caring for his heart condition advised that he should be admitted to Ignatia Hall for his first alcoholism treatment. Carl's initial laboratory studies revealed severe liver injury (acute alcoholic hepatitis), and by the third day he was visibly yellow, or jaundiced. He also started demonstrating some very bizarre behavior, including walking down the hall naked, climbing into other patients' beds while they were still in them, having difficulty deciding where he was, and using abusive language with the staff. Both medical and psychiatric consultants were called in, and Carl was transferred to a medical floor with a diagnosis of acute liver damage and hepatic encephalopathy. In simple terms, his liver was not metabolizing the protein in his diet and he was accumulating high levels of ammonia in his blood. He stayed on the medical floor for about ten days. However, his daughter insisted we evaluate him again for the Ignatia Hall program. The medical staff felt his liver was improving steadily, but he continued to have lapses of memory as well as some episodes of aberrant behavior. Nurses' notes indicated that he wandered down the hall in a seemingly aimless fashion. For these reasons, we considered Carl to have altered brain function secondary to hardening of the arteries. Our staff questioned the appropriateness of our program for this patient.

Admittedly, his thought processes remained fairly cloudy, but I was struck by how much his mental status had improved since the first time I had seen him, some ten days earlier. There are times in medicine when you have a certain feeling or play a hunch to do something in spite of the available objective evidence indicating otherwise. I took a chance and admitted Carl to our extended care program for twenty-one days. Initially, he resisted the entire idea, but I guess he felt that it might be easier to enter the program than have to face the wrath of his daughter if he didn't. Certain kinds of coercion seem to have a place in the treatment of alcoholism, an approach sometimes referred to as tough love.

What took place over the next twenty-one days was, at least in my opinion and that of the other staff members, just short of a miracle. Carl seemed to get a little better each day; he seemed to have more enthusiasm, become more active and, above all, have a much sharper mind. On the day of discharge he was literally a different man. As one of the younger staff members remarked, "This old gentleman is sharper than some of my friends." The happy ending to the story is that Carl returned to his Southern home, and the last we heard was an announcement that he was to marry his childhood sweetheart.

Unfortunately, these types of endings are not as frequent as we would hope. But to us, it reinforced the importance of a good diet, rest, and *no alcohol*. It also raised in our minds the question of how many older people are misdiagnosed as having senile psychosis, dementia, organic brain syndrome, Alzheimer's Disease, or some other type of psychiatric problem when the underlying problem is actually chronic alcoholism.

Emotional Problems and Alcoholism

When asked at admission time, at least 90 percent of our patients say they are depressed. Their depression is often intermingled with feelings of guilt, embarrassment, or just feeling angry with themselves for being where they are. According to the histories they give, these feelings of depression have been present for several weeks to several months, or even years, and appear to correlate with the periods of time when the patient was actively drinking. The degree of depression is so significant that when a psychiatric consultation is requested, three out of every ten patients are started on an antidepressant medication. The other six or seven patients usually show a lessening of the depression in a few days following the routine treatment offered all patients.

The psychiatrist's challenge is to determine whether depression is *primary* or *secondary* in origin; was the depression there before the drinking problem, or was it a result of the drinking problem? In all too many instances, it is not possible to answer this question during the eight-day treatment program; it is difficult enough to evaluate during the twenty-one-day extended treatment program. Usually, the psychiatrist makes the diagnosis of a major depressive disorder only after several months, with follow-up visits to determine whether the depression is alcohol-related or not. For the majority of patients, we find that if they follow through with a treatment plan after discharge, including aftercare, counseling, and AA meetings, as well as a good diet, rest, and no alcohol—the combination can do wonders for the mind, body, and soul, including the disappearance of depression.

On the other hand, there are some patients who show increasingly more serious psychiatric problems as they go through the withdrawal phase and each day thereafter. Perhaps two case descriptions would be helpful here. Jim, a thirty-three-year-old laborer, presented himself to the treatment center obviously drunk. He was admitted and went through the first thirty-six hours with no significant signs and symptoms of withdrawal. Then he became unmanageable, throwing things, yelling, swearing, and physically assaulting several of the female staff. His psychiatrist recommended that he be probated, that is, taken bodily to a nearby state psychiatric hospital. It took all our orderlies and some members of the local police force to accomplish this because he had become extremely violent. Later his family revealed that he had been in and out of psychiatric hospitals since he was twenty with a diagnosis of paranoid schizophrenia. The lesson to be learned: patients with serious psychiatric problems can have alcohol problems too.

Bert was a forty-two-year-old district manager for a computer firm. I first saw him about eight hours after he was admitted to our center very drunk. As I approached him in his bed, it was obvious that he was going through severe withdrawal. His tremors were so severe his entire bed was shaking and he was sweating profusely. A check revealed his pulse to be 120 beats per minute. As I extended my hand to introduce myself, he grabbed it with both hands as if hanging on for dear life. In a pleading, scared tone, the likes of which I will never forget, he said, "Doc, every time I go through withdrawal I end up in a psychiatric unit strapped to my bed in leathers (leather restraining straps) because I want to kill people!" You can be assured that this statement caught my attention, and I immediately called for a psychiatric consultation. In addition to following the standard treatment for withdrawal, the psychiatrist started the patient on an antipsychotic medication called a neuroleptic. Bert went through the rest of his withdrawal in an uneventful manner, and, much to his pleasure, we did not have to put him in a psychiatric unit in leathers. As an afternote, Bert is celebrating his third year of sobriety and is receiving the appropriate medication for his paranoid schizophrenic psychiatric condition.

These two cases demonstrate two important points: patients who have underlying psychiatric disorders can hide their disorders in part when they are drunk, and, second, patients who have an underlying psychiatric disorder can develop a second disease, alcoholism. It would appear that these patients initially drank alcohol as a form of self-medication—something to calm themselves down. However with time, the process progresses to the point where they cross the line and become physically dependent. Then one must treat not only the signs and symptoms of withdrawal, but, at the same time, the underlying psychiatric disorder. These patients are considered to have a dual diagnosis, which is to say, *two separate diseases.*

Alcohol can cause damage not only to every organ of the body, but to the mind and the spiritual well-being of any human being as well.

Tolerance and the Anesthetic Effects of Alcohol

Before going into the last stage of the disease of alcoholism—*death*—let me discuss two very important aspects of alcohol from a pharmacological point of view: alcohol as an anesthetic and the phenomenon of tolerance.

"Alcohol makes me crazy before I pass out!" I can't count the number of times I've heard this comment from younger patients (eighteen to twenty-five years of age). What are they really saying? Scientists have known for some time that alcohol acts on the cell membrane of all body cells, and especially brain cells (called neurons) by dissolving in the fat or lipid portion of the membrane. Ether, well known for its early use in anesthesia, also acts on the brain cells in this manner. We all know the Hollywood version of alcohol as an anesthetic: The mountain man staggers into town with an arrow in his chest, the local sawbones hands the patient a bottle of "red-eye" whiskey and a bullet to bite, the doc gives a mighty tug and out comes the arrow, and usually out goes the patient—passed out drunk.

I pointed out earlier that a person goes through four levels of anesthesia when undergoing a general, as opposed to local, anesthetic: 1) euphoria, 2) amnesia, 3) relaxation, and 4) death. I have just a few more comments about each of these levels in light of what we have learned about the disease of alcoholism.

1) Euphoria

This is the happy phase of drinking alcohol. We begin to lose our inhibitions and become more talkative, outgoing, and, above all, we're not hurting for anything after one or more drinks. People selling alcoholic beverages capitalize on this Happy Hour personality shift, which is one of the effects people drink to feel. Because of this type of behavior, people tend to regard alcohol as a stimulant rather than a depressant—"one or two drinks under my belt and I'm rarin' to go." Historically, it has been suggested that many great writers, Hemingway for one, did some of their greatest writing under the influence of alcohol. But alcohol is a sedative, just like the barbiturates and all other tranquilizers. Many have seen the person who is initially the life of the party as his or her blood alcohol level is rising, but when the party is at its peak this person is not to be found, because he or she is sleeping in some corner. The euphoria we see after one or more drinks, depending upon the level of one's tolerance, is believed to be due to the selective suppression of inhibitory centers of the brain. This releases the excitatory centers of the brain to function unopposed because they have not yet been suppressed. Long-time heavy drinkers do not usually experience this initial stimulatory effect because they are in a near-constant state of numbness. During this stimulatory phase of intoxication, the nerves tend to be more active and uninhibited for a short time, but then these excitatory and other centers of the brain are also suppressed in turn until the overall depressive effects of alcohol are felt. Scientists are beginning to study just why there is this difference in sensitivity among different centers of the brain.

2) Amnesia

Just as it is not uncommon for the patient in the recovery room not to remember a thing about the operation, it is common for alcoholics going through periods of blackout not to remember where they parked the car, how they wound up in another city, that they were in a fight, or were resisting arrest, or how they got black and blue with bruises all over. These kinds of things seem to happen to people who are drinking and have a blackout.

But you don't have to be an alcoholic to have a blackout—this can happen to anyone who drinks alcohol. I have been involved in numerous court cases where teenagers, in particular, have literally destroyed their future by being involved in some type of illegal activity during a blackout. Being in a blackout is not generally accepted by juries as an excuse.

3) Relaxation

During this stage of anesthesia, the muscles become relaxed to the point where the person just collapses, as well as feels no pain. This same stage is reached by some of our patients who have been engaged in excessive drinking. On several occasions I have seen a patient's body literally covered with bruises from the top of his head to the soles of his feet. When I ask what happened, the answer is something like "I fell down several flights of stairs," or "I totalled my car around a telephone pole." Yet there are no broken bones! The most likely reason is that they were so very relaxed. You usually don't break a bone unless there are resistant forces acting upon the bone through the contraction of muscles. This is why paratroopers in training are told to hit the ground relaxed. However, for every serious accident in which a drunk escapes serious injury through the relaxing effects of alcohol, there are many more cases where injuries are suffered by drinking drivers, especially those who don't wear seatbelts. Recent studies show a higher percentage of injuries to drivers under the influence of alcohol than to nondrinking drivers. And, of course, this doesn't address the likelihood of getting into an accident while drinking in the first place.

On the other side of the coin, it is very easy during this relaxation stage to fall and fracture some bone(s), especially the ribs. The drinker may not feel a thing as long as the blood alcohol is elevated, but as the sobering-up process takes place and the anesthesia is wearing off, the pain becomes very noticeable. In examining and treating any intoxicated person, one must always ascertain whether any bones are broken. We are especially careful when patients have bruises, or in those instances where someone saw them fall, because we have to consider the possibility of the sharp ends of a broken bone piercing certain organs of the body or causing further damage. In spite of the growing clamor to hold health care costs down, any patient admitted to our center with a suspicious-looking bruise or a report of a recent fall is thoroughly X-rayed to rule out any fractures. Most of the X-ray reports come back negative, but we do not want to take any chances. Besides, to do otherwise would be poor medicine.

4) Death

Street talk has it that you can't overdose with alcohol, that you get so drunk that you pass out first. This is an unfortunate misperception, particularly among younger people. You can overdose on alcohol. It depends on your age, sex, body size, tolerance and, most critically, the amount you drink and over what time period. Recently, a sixteen-year-old high school student was D.O.A. (dead on arrival) at our emergency room. The local newspaper account of the tragedy told how a group of teenagers attending a family reunion were off by themselves engaged in horseplay. In a joking spirit, someone dared one of the members to chug-a-lug a glass of 151-proof rum from the makeshift bar outside. He accepted the dare, and thirty minutes later he was dead.

The lesson to be learned from all this is that when *any* person drinks alcohol, depending on how much they drink, they can go through the same changes that occur in people undergoing general anesthesia for surgery: euphoria, amnesia, relaxation, and even death. Any person means just that, from the young child who first got drunk when he went into his dad's liquor cabinet and tasted all the bottles, to the high school senior who wanted to be one of the boys and had three beers and passed out. Even experienced drinkers who have developed a tolerance for alcohol can die from an alcohol overdose—the male nurse who took a bottle of wine to bed each night or the thirty-six-year-old house painter who—after being extricated from the twisted remains of a car—said he had no idea how much he had to drink, how he got into someone else's car, how he smashed it into a telephone pole, or how he got to the hospital.

It has been said that people who have been hypnotized will not perform any act under posthypnotic suggestion that is contrary to their morals or normal lifestyle. This is not necessarily so when one is under the influence of alcohol or any general anesthesia, depending, of course, on the level of anesthesia. There is always the possibility of reaching a level of anesthesia when drinking where you lose any sense of moral restriction or control over your own behavior and carry out acts that are not only bizarre, but in many instances against the law. The sobering fact is that after the effects of the alcohol have worn off, you may have absolutely no recollection of having done any of the things you have been accused of doing. How much do you have to drink before you feel the anesthetic effects of alcohol and start doing things that will get you into trouble?

Developing Tolerance to Alcohol

Each of us has some idea or feeling as to what our limits are in terms of drinking. It could be "One bottle of beer or glass of wine and I'm ready to go to sleep," or, at the other extreme, "Doc, I can handle a case of beer a day with no problem." Stated in terms of body chemistry, the biochemical reactions in our bodies will be influenced initially by a certain level of alcohol in our blood stream. However, over a period of time, the amount of alcohol necessary to get the same biochemical reaction is greater. This is called acquired tolerance. The more you drink, and the more months or years you drink, the more your tolerance will build, and the more beers it will take to get a buzz.

The need to drink more and more alcohol to get a desired effect is partly due to changes over a period of time in the enzymes of the liver that are responsible for breaking down (metabolizing) alcohol to carbon dioxide, water, and energy. With continuous exposure to more and more alcohol over long periods of time, these enzymes are able to break down the alcohol faster and faster. Studies have shown that the blood alcohol concentration will drop 10mg% an hour (0.010 percent) in someone who seldom drinks, and then only for a small amount of alcohol, compared to a rate of 20 to 30mg% an hour (0.020–0.030 percent) in someone who has been a heavy drinker for a long time.

The tolerance for alcohol of some of the patients admitted to our center is almost uniformly high. The blood alcohol level at the time of admission ranges from 0 to the highest we have ever recorded: 563mg/dl (milligrams per deciliter—a deciliter is a tenth of a liter, or just over 3 fluid ounces), reported as a percentage of 0.563. The average is about 169mg/dl (0.169%) at the time of admission. Most states define 100mg/dl (0.10%) as legally intoxicated if one is driving an automobile. A level of 500mg/dl (0.50%) is considered potentially fatal. People often ask me what happened to the patient with the .563% blood alcohol level, since this is regarded as probably a fatal level. Actually, it is an interesting story that illustrates a point.

Joe was a twenty-eight-year-old college student when he was admitted during the early morning hours with a blood alcohol level of 563mg%. The nursing staff reported this to me, and we instituted a series of standard orders as a precaution in case the patient started to show signs of acute alcohol toxicity. I arrived at the hospital shortly after being notified, and went immediately to the patient's room only to find it empty. The two thoughts going through my mind were that either the patient had died or he had been taken to the Intensive Care Unit with some critical problem. As it turned out, neither was the case. As I headed toward the nursing station, I passed the dining area, and there was the patient in front of a tray with at least three or four eggs, several strips of bacon, and four pieces of toast. When he saw me, he stopped eating and greeted me with slurred speech: "Hi, Doc, the food is really great in this place!" Frankly, I couldn't believe my eyes at first, because from everything I'd seen or read up to this point, this man should have been dead or close to it, not sitting up eating breakfast. Obviously he wasn't dead; he didn't even act particularly drunk at that point.

Most individuals metabolize, or burn up, alcohol at the rate of 15 to 30mg% an hour. Assuming the higher end of this range, a patient with a blood alcohol level of 563mg/dl would take three hours to reduce his blood alcohol level to even 473mg%.

I learned many things from this patient, as I do from all our patients, but two points stuck in my mind. The first lesson is that there is nothing magical about the number 500mg%. As a matter of fact, deaths have been reported for people with levels of 250mg%. You must treat each patient individually, including monitoring each one's clinical status on an almost minute-by-minute basis, and not treat him or her by the laboratory numbers. The second thing that struck me was the realization of the range or the high degree of tolerance a person can develop to alcohol. Here was a young, basically intact man with a blood alcohol level at or above the normally fatal level of toxicity calmly enjoying a hearty breakfast. I should add that four to six hours later, this man went through a very severe withdrawal, and it was only because of our excellent nursing staff that he did not get into any serious problems.

Tolerance to alcohol is beginning to take on some very important legal implications. Evidence is accumulating that some individuals with blood alcohol levels as high as 200mg% (compared to the legal limit of 100mg%) show minimal or no signs of psychomotor impairment. They seem to have developed a tolerance to alcohol to a point that in others would produce all the signs of intoxication, yet these individuals appear to be able to carry out seemingly normal muscular activities—walking a straight line, touching their finger to the end of their nose with eyes closed, and speaking coherently. Scientists are discovering that tolerance to alcohol can develop through the direct effects of alcohol on the nerve cells of the brain and the rest of the nervous system, which in turn affects muscle movement and certain types of behaviors.

Recently, we had a fashionably dressed man about fifty-five years old present himself to our admitting desk saying, "I wish to be admitted to your treatment center." This man appeared to be, and was, a high-level executive. He spoke in a mild, well-mannered voice, and had no obvious evidence of intoxication. The admitting nurse, with over eleven years' experience with alcoholic patients, suggested to the man that perhaps he had gotten off on the wrong floor, and that this was the alcoholic treatment center. His reply was "This is where I want to be, I need treatment for my drinking problem." The man was admitted to the unit, and we discovered that his blood alcohol level was 310mg%. He had a very severe withdrawal experience, ending up in the coronary care unit with a diagnosis of cardiac arrythmia. Fortunately his heart returned to a normal rhythm in three days and he needed no further cardiac treatment. He later entered an extended care program. In my last contact with him, he was celebrating his second anniversary of sobriety.

But what happens to tolerance to alcohol when one stops drinking, and how does it affect the recovering alcoholic? The final answers are not in as yet, but certain clues are being gathered. Patients who have relapsed and started drinking again after months or even years of sobriety claim, "I can't handle as much as I used to drink," or "I only had three or four drinks and I knew I was in trouble; that's why I came back in," or "I don't understand, I only drank about a quarter of a bottle of gin and look at me—I totalled my car, banged up my body, and here I am again, going through treatment."

Marvin's story is worth telling. A former marine and Vietnam veteran, he had a severe alcohol problem when he was admitted to the center for the first time. He did well in the program, and after discharge he really started working his AA program. His life was falling into place by all standards. Then one morning I got off the elevator to the center and there was Marvin with bruises all over his head and arms and, as was revealed later, all over the rest of his body. To say the least, I was surprised, but it was quite obvious he had had a relapse. At first he was very quiet and would not say much. He was obviously very ashamed and embarrassed, and what made matters worse was that he had just celebrated his first anniversary of sobriety. When he finally started talking, his biggest question was: "How did this happen to me? I swear, Doc, when the police pulled me out of the car, they found the bottle of gin, and I swear to God there was only one or two ounces missing. Now I could handle two fifths of gin a day just a year ago and still go to work. I simply can't believe that just that little bit of gin would cause me to black out and get me into all this trouble." Marvin went through the treatment program again, and once more he is doing well. The last we heard, he had enrolled in a university to get his degree and planned to go into counseling.

One of the big no-nos in the AA program for recovering alcoholics is "Don't take that first drink." The story of tolerance provides part of the reason why. I tell my patients that when they were admitted, their tolerance to alcohol was high—in the 200 to 300 or 400mg% level. Then they stopped drinking. As the period of sobriety got longer, their tolerance to alcohol became less and less. Also, they started to feel really good and life was becoming enjoyable again. Then along comes a friend who insists on buying you a beer. You refuse, because you have foremost in your mind "Don't take that first drink!" But your friend insists: "One beer won't hurt you. Hell, I remember when you and I could put away two cases a day." You think: "Yes, that's true, and besides, I feel really good, Okay, one beer."

That starts the cycle. Before our patients heard this lecture, they probably didn't know that their tolerance went down with sobriety. One beer plus a lowered tolerance and the stage of euphoria is reached very quickly. Feeling good and beginning to lose inhibitions, it's easy to order a second, a third, and a fourth beer. Before long, the person is calling us for help and being readmitted to the center. We are finding one positive trend: when our former patients relapse, they are beginning to call us sooner than they used to. Instead of going on a heavy drinking spree of weeks or months before seeking help, they are asking to be readmitted within a few days after they have had a slip or a first drink. We can't help feeling that this is a very positive sign. They are learning about alcoholism and have a much better understanding of their disease.

There is yet another dimension of tolerance, the genetic factor. Research suggests that genetic factors determine what may be called a pre-existing tolerance to alcohol. Different people seem to have different natural tolerances to alcohol which are apparent from the time they take their first drink. Many of our patients describe how when they were teenagers, or even younger, and had tried drinking for the first time some of the fellows would start acting really silly and others wouldn't feel a thing. This innate sort of tolerance may become one of our next early warning signs of alcohol-ism. And eventually we may be able to better predict whose genetic makeup will make them especially prone to develop-ing an addiction to alcohol.

Death—The Final Stage

When and why do alcoholics die? As mentioned earlier, the average age at which alcoholics will die of their disease if untreated is in their early fifties. The youngest patient we have had die in the hospital was twenty-six years old. Fred started drinking at age fourteen and entered his first alcohol treatment program at twenty-six. By the time he was admit-ted, his liver was severely damaged, so much so that we transferred him to another medical unit where he stayed for almost sixty days before he succumbed to liver failure. Although we focus on liver disease, specifically cirrhosis of the liver, as the major cause of death, alcoholics die of a wide range of causes while under the influence of alcohol. They frequently die by suicide, in automobile accidents, homi-cides, home accidents, boating accidents, and in fights, as well as from secondary damage associated with complica-tions to other organs of the body. Sadness always accompanies death, but those of us who treat alcoholics have to deal with a sense of frustration as well as sadness when a former patient dies. The frustration stems from feeling that: "Everyone else recognized that you were destroying yourself with alco-hol, why didn't you know it? Or did you, and you just didn't care? Or was it that you really didn't understand what alcohol was doing to you?"

Let me give you one last example. Pam was a twenty-nine-year-old woman who had graduated from high school and had about a year of college. She was admitted to the medical center from the emergency room with a diagnosis of terminal liver failure secondary to alcohol. She had severe ascites (accumulation of fluid in her abdomen), to the point that she looked like she was seven to eight months pregnant. Her body weight was 143 pounds at admission, compared to her normal weight of 118 pounds. She was in and out of hepatic coma, and her parents insisted that there be no heroic efforts to keep her alive with machines. Much to everyone's surprise, she began to recover to the point where she would walk around the floor and her mental status began to clear. At this time, the doctors on the unit urged her to enter the alcoholism treatment program. The staff, myself included, were almost dumbfounded that this rather bright young lady refused to accept the fact that alcohol, namely the ten to twelve beers she had been drinking on an almost daily basis, was responsible for the condition of her liver. As it turned out, both her parents were alcoholics and drank beer daily as well. This proved to be the basis for her skepticism that beer could be the problem. "Mom and Dad drink as much beer as I do, and they are in their sixties and don't have any liver problems," she insisted. The saddest part of this sad situation is that this woman was not even aware that she was destroying herself. As things worked out, through the treatment program of education and persuasion, she began to realize what alcohol can do to your body and had already done to hers. Because of her case and countless others like it, I am becoming increasingly convinced that ignorance about the effects of alcohol, and the disease of alcoholism in general, plays a much greater role in this widespread problem than we are prepared to accept.

SEVEN

Who Is An Alcoholic?

"Hi, my name is _____ and I'm an alcoholic" is the traditional opening line of the person giving the lead (or talk) at an AA meeting. This type of introduction is important, not only because it reflects a person's acceptance of having the disease of alcoholism, but—just as important—because it reflects having the courage to share one's story with family, friends, and even total strangers. Unsaid in this opening line is the pain, torment, confusion, anger, guilt, and embarrassment that was experienced before reaching the point of accepting the fact that "I am an alcoholic." But this usually unfolds during the course of the lead.

"When was the first time you ever recognized that you had a problem with alcohol, or do you?" I ask all patients admitted to our center. Their responses to this and other background questions have an important bearing on the diagnosis and treatment. About eight out of ten patients will answer without a moment's hesitation, "I knew I had a problem for the past five or six years," or "I knew I had a problem for the past several years, but only during the past two or three weeks did I face up to it," or "I finally realized yesterday that I had a problem when my wife and two daughters packed their suitcases and left me alone in the house after I had come home drunk again."

I often sense in the tone of voice or looks of disbelief the unspoken thought, "Of course I have a problem, you fool, why else would I be here?" The fact that these individuals voluntarily presented themselves to a treatment center shows a significant level of acceptance of a drinking problem—a kind of self-diagnosis if you will—and above all, a breaking down of the *denial* that a drinking problem exists. Whether the denial of the problem is the result of alcohol acting on the brain's chemistry, or whether it comes from a sense of shame, embarrassment, or fear of looking weak to others, is not important for the moment. The usual course of action is to ignore the existence of a drinking problem, play it down, or just keep it in the closet. The simple phrase "My name is _____ and I'm an alcoholic" cuts cleanly through this tangle of denial and coverup.

How do the remaining two patients out of ten react to the question, "When was the first time you ever recognized you had a problem with alcohol, or do you?" Invariably, there is a characteristic hesitation and often a turning away of their gaze as I ask the question. The pause in answering and the shift in the gaze has become for me a preface to the statement that will follow—"I really don't think I have a problem with alcohol," said in many different ways. The pause makes it appear that the person is taking a moment to think something like: "Well, here I am in an alcohol treatment center that I entered voluntarily. This must mean something is wrong, yet I just don't believe I have a drinking problem." Some of the answers that follow the pause include:

"My wife says I drink too much and that I need treatment, so I came in to keep peace in my family."

"My husband and children feel I need help, but I really don't drink that much."

"My boss warned me yesterday that I better get some help, but I never drink on the job."

"I don't have a problem. That darned cop was just waiting outside the bar for someone to come out so he could give them a ticket for DWI."

"My lawyer said it would look good on my record if I went through a treatment program before I went to court for my second DWI."

"The judge ordered me into treatment because I got a little wild the last time I was drinking."

These same patients, unlike the other eight out of ten who freely admit to having a problem, will more often than not show no significant symptoms of physical dependence or withdrawal. When they see some of their fellow patients who have crossed the line to physical dependency experiencing the shakes, nausea, and sweating, or hear some of the more bizarre tales of drinking experiences, their self-comparison leads them to the conclusion that they really don't have a drinking problem: "Oh, I drink once in a while, but nothing like those other guys..."

As you might suspect, the level of denial in this group of patients is very high. They will cling to their denial even in the face of serious medical complications. The most important challenge in treating this type of patient is to break through this denial. It is a point in our favor that they at least took a first step in entering a treatment program. But what about the thousands of other people experiencing the same types of problems who have not come to the point of accepting the presence of a problem, let alone admitting themselves to a treatment center? Unfortunately, in all too many circumstances, these drinkers will go to the hospital at some point because of the damaging effects of alcohol to the liver, heart, brain, stomach, or lungs—whatever organ is most affected. And yet even at that stage, when excessive drinking has clearly taken its toll on one or more vital organs, it is often most difficult to convince anyone that the damage was due to their drinking.

At a recent meeting of experts in the field of alcoholism, one of the speakers, an epidemiologist, asked what appeared to be a very simple question in discussing the prevalence of alcoholism in the United States: "Who should I count?" The obvious answer would seem to be anyone who has a drinking problem. But this is easier said than done. How do you define alcoholism, or what tests would you carry out to make the diagnosis? Few would have a problem in diagnosing alcoholism when the person is obviously intoxicated and within a few hours begins to have the shakes, a rapid pulse, nausea, sweating, headaches, hallucinations, and possibly even a seizure. Alcoholism is easy to see once the line of physical dependency has been crossed. It is fairly simple to diagnose alcoholism in a patient who has a severe liver injury that appears to be related to alcohol intake, whether the patient acknowledges that he or she has a drinking problem or not. But what about the person who checks into a treatment center by court order because of a second or third DWI? Should this person be counted as an alcoholic? I can assure you that the individual in 99 percent of these cases will at least initially reject the idea: "I haven't had a drink in three months since I got the DWI," or "I don't have a problem like these other patients; I feel great." So who *should* the epidemiologist count? Counters and computers want "yes" or "no" answers, and not maybes.

Medicine is a long, long way from being an exact science. The art of clinical judgement with all the blind spots and personal biases of the physician is still the cornerstone of the practice of medicine. All medical problems cannot be reduced to a black or white diagnosis, in spite of today's many advanced diagnostic tools. There is still a vast grey area where the doctor has to rely on clinical judgement to arrive at a diagnosis. And at this stage of our knowledge of the disease, alcoholism in its early stages is still a "judgement call." It is almost impossible to identify the early phases of the disease definitely enough to say that this person is an alcoholic and that person just drank too much. Alcoholism is not alone in this category of difficult-to-diagnose, progressive diseases. The progression of any such disease is like the dripping of a leaky faucet: it will drip 24 hours a day, 7 days a week, 365 days of the year, until the buildup of rust or an increase in the dripping moves someone to do something about it. So it is with all chronic diseases; they tend to proceed continuously most of the time, slowly at first, with hardly any noticeable changes to the individual or those around him, until a level of trouble or damage is reached that causes pain or swelling or skin color changes, to name a few possible signs or symptoms. There may be pauses in the process, a remission, due to the prescribed form of treatment, or possibly it happens spontaneously for reasons yet unknown.

Ok! This may all be very interesting and important to understand, but the question remains, "Who do I count?" Besides, if I don't know who to count, then practically speaking, I don't know who to treat. Well, physicians are very practical-minded people, and to deal with this type of problem, they take this continuous and progressive process and start dividing it up into phases or stages by drawing lines or creating pigeonholes with names attached in order to classify the stages. This is what we tried to do with the proposed "working model" of the disease set forth earlier: Exposure → Social Drinker → Impulsive Drinker → Addictive Drinker (Recreational Drinker, Psychologically Dependent Drinker, or Compulsive Drinker) → Physical Dependency → Medical Complications and Death.

Now comes the difficult question: where should we draw the lines between these different phases to distinguish the nonalcoholic from the alcoholic? Those who lean toward the moralistic approach say to draw the line between those who never touched a drop of alcohol and those who drink, regardless of the amount or frequency. Others would argue that only those who have crossed the line to physical dependency should be diagnosed as alcoholic. Still others would argue that the line should be drawn between those for whom alcohol has caused no problem ("He goes to work every day, he doesn't mistreat me") and those for whom it has, regardless of the amount or frequency.

I think it's possible to look at the same exact situation and come up with very different conclusions. Therefore, I think it would help to look at another chronic disease like diabetes mellitus that has been studied extensively and which doesn't have such ingrained prejudices and social ramifications to see how the dividing lines have been established, and then make some comparisons with alcoholism. There are actually some sound biological reasons for this comparison. In diabetes, for example, excess *formaldehyde* is formed from the metabolism of sugars, while an excess of *acetaldehyde* is produced in alcoholism—two very similar chemicals.

Diabetes mellitus or, as some patients refer to it, sugar in the blood or sugar in the urine is just that. The diabetic has an elevated blood sugar level compared to the normal population. Sometimes the blood sugar is so high that it spills over into the urine. These abnormal levels of sugar in the blood and urine are related to the amount of insulin that the individual's pancreas is secreting into the blood steam. *High levels of insulin equal low blood sugar levels, and low levels of insulin equal high blood sugar levels.* Since we can measure these blood glucose levels very accurately, it has been simpler to draw the lines in the progression of this disease. At the risk of oversimplifying a complicated disease that is potentially very dangerous if left untreated, let me show you how the lines were drawn between the progressive phases of diabetes:

Patient I—On a routine visit to the doctor's office, laboratory tests showed an elevated blood sugar level. The patient had been under a great deal of stress or had had the flu for the past several weeks. He had a repeat study done a month later and the results were normal. No treatment was required.

Patient II—Again, a person showed an elevated level of

blood sugar, but on repeated tests it remained elevated. However, by controlling the number of calories and types of food in the *diet*, the blood sugar level returned to normal values.

Patient III—The third patient had an elevated blood sugar level that tested high even when placed on a controlled diet. However, taking a pill plus sticking to the diet helped bring the blood sugar level back into the normal range.

Patient IV—The patient's elevated blood sugar level remained high even with a specific diet and pills. However, taking insulin by regular injections caused the blood sugar level to return to the normal range.

Patient V—The patient's persistent elevated blood sugar level returned to normal using a combination of diet, pills, and insulin, but damage had already occurred in the blood vessels of the heart, the kidney, the retina of the eye, or the feet.

Now, if our expert epidemiologist asked the same question about diabetics as he asked about alcoholics—"Who should we count?"—the answer would be based on many years of scientific investigation and widespread clinical experience. The dividing line between the nondiabetic and diabetic falls between Patient I and Patient II. Therefore, Patients II, III, IV, and V would all be counted as diabetics. But another line is drawn between Patient III and Patient IV. We call Patients IV and V Type 1 insulin-dependent diabetics, as compared to Patients II and III, who are called Type II noninsulin-dependent diabetics. However, diabetes is a progressive disease; it gets worse if left untreated. The Type I patients will probably have to take insulin for the rest of their lives, and the Type II patients can cross the line and become Type I diabetics if the disease progresses in spite of therapy, or more likely, if the therapy is not followed carefully. As seemingly neat and clear-cut as these divisions may appear, we must always remember that the lines are artificial, made up for the convenience of medical practitioners, and that many individuals fall on the boundary lines, with one foot on each side, or into a grey area.

Again at the risk of oversimplifying a very complicated disease, let me compare the stages of alcoholism to diabetes using a similar yardstick.

Patient I could be compared to the social and impulsive drinker. Unplanned episodes of excessive alcohol intake and feeling the effects can cause an occasional high blood alcohol level that is not likely to be repeated very often.

Patient II could be compared to the recreational drinker. With intentional, repeated episodes of partying and seeking the effects of alcohol, the blood alcohol level is repeatedly elevated. But there may be days, weeks, or even months between episodes, and by recognizing the problem, particularly after experiencing repeated hangovers, the blood alcohol level can be controlled. Patient II can easily control his or her blood alcohol level by regulating intake, or diet.

Patient III could be compared to the psychologically dependent drinker who engages in a consistent and persistent pattern of drinking, be it daily or weekly (weekends), because of an underlying emotional or even physical pain. This person, in addition to regulating his or her intake (diet) of alcohol, requires a "pill" in the form of professional counseling, psychotherapy, psychotropic medications, or support group meetings such as AA for the underlying emotional problem, or appropriate medical therapy in the case of underlying physical complaints.

Patient IV could be compared to the person who is physically dependent on alcohol, who has crossed the line of alcohol dependence. Unlike other patients (like the recreational drinker) who respond to regulating their intake (diet) of alcohol, and who can manage with some sort of appropriate psychological support through counseling or AA, this patient has lost the option of regulating the intake and must abstain from alcohol for the rest of his or her life. It will be necessary to continue abstinence in order to avoid the horrendous experiences of withdrawal from alcohol. Remember, "A pickle can never become a cucumber again."

Finally, *Patient V* could be compared to the person with severe medical complications secondary to drinking, whether they are physically dependent or not physically dependent. Their treatment, in addition to a no-alcohol diet and psychological and emotional support, must include some medical attention for the parts of the body that have been damaged by alcohol.

However, I should reiterate that medical complications such as damage to the liver can occur in individuals who are not addicted to alcohol—the social and impulsive drinkers, for instance. Irrespective of the pattern of drinking, the toxic effects of acetaldehyde, which results when the body breaks down the alcohol it has consumed, can cause damage depending on the amount of alcohol intake and the duration.

You may have noticed that no comparison has been made between the diabetic and the compulsive drinker. Let me illustrate the point by telling you about John. John is now forty years old and was treated in our center ten years ago.

After his discharge from our program, he became very active in Alcoholics Anonymous and worked his program very faithfully and sincerely. To date he has had ten years of sobriety.

John attended one of my Tuesday afternoon talks as an AA visitor when I first became director of Ignatia Hall and my knowledge and understanding of the disease were just beginning to grow. He became very upset at the point in my talk when I implied that only those who had crossed the line to physical dependency were alcoholics. He argued: "I was an alcoholic at least ten years before I came into treatment ten years ago, and not once did I ever experience any problems with withdrawal when I stopped drinking." My first reaction was one of doubt, and we engaged in a discussion that some would have classified as an argument. When calmness was restored, we talked about his drinking history for several hours. His own words best describe his case:

"I would go out drinking with the boys after I graduated from high school. When everyone else was ready to go home when the bar was closing, I was still putting them down with no desire or intention of stopping. In fact, I would finish off three or four more beers on the way home in the back seat of the car. The next morning I would get up not feeling the best, but I would go off to work. After eight hours on the job I might repeat the same pattern, or I might skip a night or two. The thing that amazed me was that it was almost impossible for me to have one beer and walk away. One beer always led to another, and another, and another, and it seemed like I just couldn't stop. This pattern continued into my marriage. My wife used to tell me I reminded her of an aunt who would open a box of chocolates and continue eating them until they were all gone, and then she would be looking for more."

John's wife was becoming increasingly annoyed and angry because he would never make it home after work, the dinner would get cold, and the children were always waiting for their daddy. However, she was always quick to add: "He is a good husband and provider. He would always go to work every day and never mistreated me." In any event, he entered our treatment facility ten years ago to keep peace in the family. As mentioned earlier, he became very active in AA after his discharge and has maintained his sobriety to the present day. Several other patients have told me very similar stories, which leads me to believe that there are compulsive drinkers who have not, or do not, cross the line of physical dependency. One could argue that this would eventually happen if the compulsive drinker continued to drink, or that this represented some unique type of genetic predisposition, or even some unique type of activity of the so-called reward or "happy" center of the brain. Whatever the reason, at least for the present, I will assume that there are some compulsive drinkers who are not and do not become physically dependent on alcohol and yet appear to have an uncontrollable craving for alcohol.

Whether a compulsive drinker is or is not physically dependent on alcohol as we have described it, one is tempted to speak of this person as the true or pure alcoholic. A significant number of these patients, when asked "When was the first time you recognized you had a problem with alcohol, or do you?", will answer with barely a moment's hestitation: "When I took my first drink of alcohol X numbers of years ago. I recognized it by the way I felt and the way I acted. I was different from my friends."

Well, are we now ready to start counting who are alcoholics? If we use the comparison between the stages of diabetes (patients II through V) and the proposed stages of alcoholism, then the recreational drinker, the psychologically dependent drinker, the compulsive drinker, the physically dependent drinker, and the person who has developed severe medical complications would be counted as alcoholics. Some would say this is a very reasonable division, but I feel it leaves a lot of grey areas.

For example, I recently visited the Georgetown area of our nation's capitol. It was Friday night, and the sidewalks were literally overflowing with people—local college students, tourists, and others. It seemed like every other business establishment on the main drag was a bar and/or a restaurant. It was obvious just by watching the crowd that a lot of alcohol was being consumed. I happened to notice two young people passed out in their cars. While walking a distance of six to seven blocks, I saw at least three or four people swaying or staggering down the street, either obnoxiously or not, and some were singing or shouting at the tops of their voices either obscenities or humorous remarks. The majority of the people in the crowd were just walking along taking in the sights. I asked one waiter about the tipsy street scene and the waiter shrugged and said: "They're just having fun. They do this every weekend." Indeed, I think we could find a repetition of this T.G.I.F. phenomenon (Thank God It's Friday—I don't have to go to work or classes tomorrow) in numerous communities throughout the nation.

If we were to start counting the alcoholics in this Friday night street scene using the above criteria the number would undoubtedly be rather high. The denial rate, however, would probably be close to 100 percent; after all, "we're just having a good time." Yet a significant number of these partiers will end up in alcohol treatment centers physically dependent on alcohol, with or without damage to their organs. But the question remains, which ones?

The obvious missing ingredient is some type of objective evidence—something we can measure, a number that all could agree upon, like a blood glucose level—rather than moral or behavioral judgements ("He's drunk!") or opinions ("Aw, he's just having fun!"). Unfortunately, we have no laboratory test, as of today, that will permit us to make a definite diagnosis of alcoholism, at least in the early stages of the disease. If we had such a test, it might be possible to prevent the later stages of the disease from ever developing. It would certainly make the alcoholic's main defense—denial—less convincing.

You may be wondering why we don't just measure the blood alcohol concentrations (BAC) as we measured the blood glucose levels to make the diagnosis of diabetes. After all, the law says that a blood alcohol level of 0.100grams% or 100mg% makes one legally intoxicated.

If you are driving a car with a blood alcohol level of 0.100gm% or higher, you can be cited for driving while intoxicated (DWI) or driving under the influence (DUI). But does this make one an alcoholic? It means that the person has become mentally and physically impaired by the anesthetic effects of alcohol to the point that he or she is a hazard to themselves as well as to innocent bystanders.

Viewed in another way, glucose, taken into the body, can be stored in the liver and the muscles as glycogen (animal starch) and is kept at a relatively constant level in the blood stream by the insulin secreted by the pancreas to keep the body's machinery working smoothly. Alcohol, on the other hand, is not stored in the body at all, but as fast as it is absorbed, is broken down. The rate averages between 10 to 30mg% per hour as measured in the blood stream. A person with a BAC of .100gm% (100mg%) could have a 0 value in as short a time as three hours and be relatively sober. This does not guarantee that he won't be experiencing the horrors of a hangover, which comes from the breakdown product of alcohol, acetaldehyde. The BACs of patients admitted to our treatment center range from 0 to .563gm% with an average of .169gm%. BACs can be misleading, because a patient with an admission level of 0 may be in a severe stage of withdrawal, as compared to the fellow who is admitted with a level of .150gm%, who may be obviously intoxicated, but shows no evidence of going through withdrawal or the physical features of dependency. His story might indeed be true: "I had three or four beers just before I came in here to start the court-ordered treatment following my second DWI; otherwise, I haven't had anything to drink for three or four weeks." However, as a general rule, any patient admitted with a blood alcohol level of .150gm% or higher and a history of daily drinking will almost certainly show withdrawal signs and symptoms in a matter of several hours, whether he appears intoxicated or not at this BAC. Tolerance is a factor here.

I hope continued research will eventually provide us with some type of chemical marker in the blood or urine that will permit us to diagnose alcoholism at the earliest, as well as the later stages, of the disease process. This would considerably reduce the grey area in determining who is an alcoholic. Exciting results from several laboratories in the past few years have focused attention on the breakdown product of alcohol in the liver—acetaldehyde. This potentially toxic chemical circulates in the blood stream in three forms: 1) free, 2) reversibly bound, and 3) irreversibly bound to the hemoglobin of the red blood cells. Our recent studies show that the free form disappears from the blood in a matter of hours, similar to the disappearance rate of alcohol from the blood. However, the reversibly bound acetaldehyde persists in the blood at significant levels for periods up to two weeks, and the irreversibly bound form may remain in the blood stream for months. These results appear to offer a unique opportunity to determine an individual's intake of alcohol for weeks and possibly months prior to testing. This makes it possible to monitor an individual's recovery more objectively by being able to determine whether he or she is drinking or abstaining.

Scientists have also found that acetaldehyde combines with certain chemicals of the brain called neurotransmitters to form a complex molecule called tetrahydroisoquinolone, THIQ for short, and that patients physically dependent on alcohol show higher levels of THIQs in the urine than nonalcoholics. Some researchers have suggested that a specific gene for alcoholism controls the formation of THIQs which, in turn, causes the craving for alcohol in some people and not in others. There are still many questions about these studies, but these and other types of encouraging research results highlight the need for even greater federal, state, private, and even individual financial support.

In the meantime, psychologists and social researchers have attempted to measure behavioral changes to give an indication of drinking behavior and alcoholism. Their scales can be helpful in assessing the severity of the disease in those instances where physical dependency has not yet developed. One of the simplest of the behavioral questionnaires is called the CAGE test. This test consists of four yes-or-no questions:

C Have you ever thought of *cutting down* on your drinking?

A Do you get *angry* when someone comments on your drinking?

G Do you ever feel *guilty* about your drinking?

E Do you ever need a drink in the morning to settle your nerves (an *eyeopener*)?

Anyone who answers two or more of the questions with a "yes" should consider the possibility of having a drinking problem and seek further evaluation and assessment. If one answers all four questions "yes," that person can be considered as having developed the disease of alcoholism.

Of course, one shortcoming of any of these questionnaire-type diagnostic tools is the honesty or candor of the patient in answering the questions. A patient in denial could answer all four questions "no" even though one or more of them should have been answered "yes." Also, we have found that patients under the influence will answer two or three questions "no" at the time of admission, then answer all four questions "yes" after their discharge eight days later. In spite of the shortcomings, these questionnaires give us one more opportunity to screen, assess, and evaluate the patient in arriving at the diagnosis of alcoholism.

In our treatment center we place a great deal of emphasis on the warning signs described in chapter four. By taking a detailed history from each of more than 5,000 patients, we began to see a common pattern of psychosocial features, medical signs, and symptoms that characterized the physically dependent patient. This list of thirteen characteristics could undoubtedly be expanded, but it serves our purpose well in evaluating those patients who have been admitted to our center in a state of denial about an alcohol problem. During the hour spent with each patient while doing the admission medical history and physical examination, only six questions are asked about drinking behavior. Instead of asking "Why did you start drinking?" or "Do you drink alone?" we focus on factual and objective medical information. The medical history we obtain proves to be complete, consistent, and valid almost 100 percent of the time, as later confirmed by the patient's physician, family, and friends. On the other hand, the drinking behavior information proves to be incomplete, inconsistent, and invalid about 70 to 80 percent of the time when the same questions are asked of the spouse, employer, or friend. An example of how the warning-signs list can be used may be helpful at this point.

Rick is a forty-three-year-old successful businessman. His story goes like this:

"Oh, I have a few beers on my way home from work a couple times a week, but I'm under stress all day long and I have to relax. What really gets me though is that my wife starts bitching as soon as I come through the door—'You've been drinking!' Big deal, two or three beers! Yes, I went to a counselor, but only to please my wife. It was a joke and a waste of time and money. I only agreed to come to the hospital to get her off my back. I'm not an alcoholic. God, I look at these other patients and listen to their stories—boy, they really have a drinking problem. Hey, Doc, I haven't had a drink since Wednesday [six days ago] and I never drank in the morning or at work and have never had the shakes."

Let's look at Rick's medical assessment. Of the warning signs on the list, I have only mentioned the ones that were answered with pertinent information:

1. History of blackouts. "Several times I went out with the boys and the next morning I had no idea how I got home or where I left my car."
2. History of arrests. "About three years ago I was stopped by the police after a few beers, but through connections, they dropped the DWI charge."
3. History of marital discord. "My wife is always complaining about something. I drink too much or I'm never home or I spend too much money on beer. It goes on and on."
4. History of hypertension. "A couple of times I visited my family doctor and he told me my blood pressure was high. He didn't prescribe any medicines, but told me to lose weight and cut down on my drinking."
5. History of peptic ulcer disease. "A year ago or so I was told I had an ulcer. I was given some medicine and told to lay off spicy foods and alcohol."
6. History of palpitations. "Several times I have gone to bed after a party or bowling with the guys where we all were drinking and it felt like my heart was going to jump out of my chest."

7. History of diarrhea. "Yes, there were quite a few times I had diarrhea the next morning but I thought it was because of all the beer [liquid] I drank."

8. History of decreased libido. "Oh, my sex life isn't like it used to be when I was twenty years old, but Doc, I'm forty-three years old now. Yes, I can have an erection, but after having a few beers I just can't perform like I used to. Actually, it embarrasses me the next day."

9. History of depression. "I have lots of mood swings lately. It seems that one minute I'm real anxious and irritable and the next minute I'm down and just don't give a damn. If I drink a few beers I feel better."

10. Genetic history. "My mother told me that my dad had a real drinking problem when he was younger, but I haven't seen my dad take a drink in ten or fifteen years. My mother? She never touched a drop in her life."

When I sat down with Rick and reviewed all this information, plus the laboratory finding of some evidence of mild liver injury, and discussed what it all meant, he sat there in silence just shaking his head. During the remaining days in the center, the staff reported that Rick was participating more in groups, sharing feelings with other patients, making arrangements to have an AA sponsor, and also planning to attend AA meetings upon discharge. On the exit interview Rick appeared a completely different person. Smiling, more relaxed, more open with feelings, his parting words were: "Thanks a million, Doc, to you and the staff. It's going to be real hard at times to accept it, but I know that I am an alcoholic!"

EIGHT

Alcoholism and Women

Alcoholism has long been regarded as a man's disease, with most recent statistics showing a four-to-one ratio of males over females. Recently, more is being written about alcoholism in women. One explanation for the assumed lower incidence in the female population is because the traditional homemaker role allowed for becoming a closet-type drinker. Now, as women have left the privacy of their homes to join the work force in increasing numbers, they are more visible, and some predict that as this hidden drinking becomes more public we will no longer see alcoholism as a predominantly male disease. St. Thomas Medical Center embarked on a long-term study to watch for trends in the incidence of alcoholism in women. Ignatia Hall, unlike many alcoholism treatment centers that are selective about who is admitted or not admitted based on ability to pay, has a patient population group that is a cross-sectional representation of the socioeconomic groups of our community, ranging from the indigent (nonpaying) to the prosperous.

Since 1978 the percentage of women admitted to our center stayed amazingly close to 18 percent until 1986. During the past five years, we have seen the number of women admitted to our center increase to 32 percent of the admissions. The ratio shifted from four to one to about three to one. We have no explanation for this recent increase in female patients.

Overall, I have found little or no difference in the psychosocial and medical histories between the female and the male patients admitted to our center. The percent being admitted for their first treatment for the disease is strikingly similar: 32 percent for females and 31 percent for males. Their average age on first admission is also similar: women average 35.1 years and males 34.7 years. And the overall range for all admissions is also the same: women eighteen to eighty-eight years and men eighteen to eighty-nine years. There is a slight increase in the number of women who have been admitted to a psychiatric unit prior to their admission to our center, but it is not all that dramatic: 28 percent for the females and 20 percent for the males. The women usually had their first drink of alcohol at a later average age— seventeen years compared to twelve years for the males. Fewer women attended AA meetings before their admission to our center. However, approximately 90 percent of the women acknowledged that they had a drinking problem, while approximately 80 percent of men admitted that they had a problem on admission.

The frequency of divorce was definitely less among the woman patients, but the incidence of women having an alcoholic spouse was greater. I would frequently hear the comment: "I would drink right along with my husband."

The number of arrests for public intoxication, disorderly conduct, and DWIs were fewer for the women, but at least 15 percent of our female patients had one or more alcohol-related arrests. The same pattern was found for the number of times a woman was fired or warned on the job because of drinking as compared to men, and between 5 to 10 percent lost their jobs because of alcohol.

The medical picture is also very similar between male and female patients. Women had their share of broken bones resulting from falls when they were drinking. Fewer women than men were treated for hypertension and ulcers, but women experienced alcohol-related palpitations of the heart, loss of appetite, morning vomiting and/or dry heaves, diarrhea, numbness and tingling of the hands and feet, as well as depression—all in about the same frequency as the men. The woman patient's response to the question "How does drinking affect your sexual activity or interest?" was interesting. Under age thirty, like their male counterparts, the usual answer was something like "My sexual desires go way up!" Over thirty years of age, the male will usually answer with a more or less frustrated tone in his voice, "It goes way down—when I drink, sex is the last thing on my mind, but even if the desire is there, I can't perform." The over-thirty woman, on the other hand, will almost always just shrug her shoulders, as if sex hasn't been a priority in her life for some time.

There is no difference in smoking habits between male and female patients—99 percent smoke cigarettes—and both groups usually comment, "When I drink, I smoke two or three times as much." Women's preferences for different types of alcoholic beverages are somewhat different than men's. Men prefer beer, whiskey, wine, and vodka in that order, but women appear to have a greater preference for liqueurs like peppermint schnapps, cognac, and brandy. They also drink beer, whiskey, wine, and vodka in no specific order of preference.

As pointed out earlier, approximately one-half (52 percent of all male patients answer "yes!" when asked, "As far as you know, did your father ever have, or has now, a drinking problem?" Women answer "yes" to the question about 50 percent of the time. Men and women asked the same question about their mothers answer "yes!" 21 and 20 percent respectively.

We take a blood alcohol level of all patients within one hour of admission. I have found no significant differences between the blood alcohol levels of the two groups (average BAC is 162mg% versus 163mg%, and the percent of patients with a negative blood alcohol level is 33 percent versus 35 percent).

As far as medical complications are concerned, there are no major comparative differences. Since 99 percent of the female patients also smoke, they have developed a high incidence of emphysema. Women patients have also developed a significant degree of liver injury (alcoholic hepatitis). Based on liver function tests, it would appear that overall women have shown a much greater degree of liver damage when compared to men of comparable age and period of drinking. This has been explained, in part, by the differences in average body size, fat content, and total water content. Women, compared to men of the same size, have a smaller total volume of water in the body. This suggests that if both drink the same amount of alcohol, it will be more diluted in the male body. This, then, could result in more alcohol damage in the woman from equal amounts of alcohol.

Scientists have recently uncovered an additional factor to explain this male/female difference. It has been reported that males have a higher concentration of an enzyme that breaks down alcohol than do women. This suggests that if a male and a female drink the same amount, the female will have a higher blood alcohol level.

Peripheral neuropathy, or numbness and tingling in the hands and feet usually associated with a vitamin B-complex deficiency, tends to be a more common complaint in women than in men. During the past year, two out of a total of one hundred eighty women patients were diagnosed as having breast cancer. It has been suggested that estrogen-like chemicals (phytoestrogens) in certain alcoholic beverages may cause an increased occurrence of breast cancer in alcoholic women. Our number of patients is too small to comment on this point.

Women go through the same misery, pain, and discomfort as men when coming off alcohol and going through the withdrawal phase of physical dependency. They shake just as hard with the tremors, they hallucinate, and they can have seizures every bit as severe as those of the men. There does appear to be a greater incidence of cross-addiction in women, especially with tranquilizers like Valium and Librium.

What does all this mean? Nothing really surprising or new. Alcoholism in women is like alcoholism in men. It's the same disease, just as diabetes is the same disease in either men or women, with the usual individual variations.

But how do women react to or cope with their disease? Now some significant differences come out. Recently, I overheard a discussion in one of the group therapy sessions where one of the female patients remarked, "Why is it that when one of you fellows plays around with other women you are called a playboy, but when a woman plays around with men she is called a slut or a whore?" The double standard of sexism certainly occurs in the population of our treatment center as elsewhere in society. We are still in the process of establishing separate facilities for men and women, because it is especially true during the acute withdrawal phase that the woman patient, in addition to being physically sick and at her lowest level of self-worth, is also emotionally devastated by being in this condition in front of all the men. Whenever feasible, we have separate group therapy sessions for men and women. We have come to learn how reluctant most women are to speak up in a mixed group. In our all-female groups, our counselors hear things that our patients have been suppressing for years. Sadly, it is not infrequent for a female patient to reveal for the first time in her life something she has been carrying around for ten, twenty, or thirty or more years—"My alcoholic father sexually abused me when I was a little girl."

With the same regimen as we prescribe for men, rest, a good diet, vitamins, no alcohol, and regular counseling and education programs, I have seen remarkable transformations in our female patients' attitudes. They often go from intensely negative to increasingly positive, and sometimes smile more than they have in years after relieving themselves of one or more of these emotional burdens. In addition to experiencing all the pain and discomfort of the disease of alcoholism, women have to deal with their own and the public's stereotyped images of the female alcoholic. The female alcoholic tends to be viewed as the lowest of the low. I believe that much more attention and resources need to be focused on the problems of the female alcoholic, and that she must be treated like the male in all respects. After all, they have the same disease!

NINE

Stuporous, Stupid, and Secretive Denial

"Ted, have you ever been treated for alcoholism before?"

"No!"

"Have you ever had a convulsion?"

"No!"

"Have you ever had hallucinations?"

"No!"

"Have you ever had a blackout?"

"No, what's that?"

"A blackout is when you don't remember what you did or were doing the night before, like when you wake up the next morning after drinking and you are not sure how you got home, let alone got into bed, or you don't remember where you parked the car."

"No, never had that problem."

"Have you ever had psychiatric treatment?"

"No, I'm not crazy!"

"Have you ever been arrested for DWI or public intoxication?"

"No!"

"Have you ever been fired or warned on the job about your drinking?"

"No, never missed a day of work in my *life*. Besides, I never drink on the job."

"Ted, do you think you have a drinking problem?"

"Not really. Oh, I drink a little bit. I'm not an alcoholic!"

Follow-up interviews with Ted's wife and best friend revealed that the answers to essentially all of the above questions should have been "yes." Some would call Ted's behavior a striking example of denial of a drinking problem, or just plain lying. I often hear some of the old-timers in AA refer to alcoholics as con artists, liars, or manipulators. Frankly, I believe this is a case of unfortunate and unfair labeling. Let's look at Ted's case a little more closely.

Ted's wife discovered him passed out on the floor next to his bed one night with blood all over his face. Frantically, she called Ted's best friend and together they were able to rouse him, get him cleaned up a little, dressed, and headed for the hospital emergency room. By the time they arrived at the hospital, Ted was pretty much awake and talked with the emergency room physician, who described his clinical condition as alert and oriented with no major medical problems. However, the laboratory findings told the tale—Ted's blood alcohol level was 463mg% (500mg% and higher is considered by many as potentially fatal), and all of his liver function tests indicated significant liver injury. On the recommendation of the physician, and after considerable urging from his wife and friend, Ted very begrudgingly agreed to enter our alcohol treatment center that night.

The question-and-answer dialogue quoted earlier took

place the next morning, while Ted was unable to get out of his bed because of the shakes and tremors. He continued to complain of shortness of breath and profuse sweating. He had such a severe case of diarrhea that he soiled his bedclothes as well as the bed linens several times during the next two days. He also had recurrent bouts of the dry heaves. All in all, he was one big mess, a classic case of severe alcohol withdrawal. In spite of being in this miserable condition, he insisted that he really didn't have a drinking problem. Rather, he insisted that all these happenings were caused by stress brought on by a job demotion (this took place a year earlier), financial problems, and the fact that his wife had breast cancer (she did have surgery performed approximately ten years ago and, by all criteria, was free of cancer). Ted was in a state of denial.

Very significantly, as each day passed in treatment and the tremors decreased, as did the sweating, dry heaves, and diarrhea, Ted began to respond to these same questions in the affirmative:

"Yes, I have had numerous blackouts."

"Yes, I entered a treatment center about two years ago, but left after a couple of days because it was dirty."

"Yes, I was arrested once about ten years ago for public intoxication, but the charge was dropped because I knew the chief of police."

"Yes, my boss mentioned several times to me a year or two ago that I should cut down on my drinking."

"Yes, I had a nervous breakdown about ten years ago when my wife was told she had breast cancer. I spent about three weeks in a psychiatric unit."

During the eighth day of hospitalization, which is the usual endpoint for completing the acute treatment phase of the program, Ted insisted that he was ready to go home. "I'm feeling great. Haven't felt like this in years. You can bet I'll never drink again. Doc, I promise you, you will never see me again as a patient. I will never touch another drop in my life."

In spite of all these encouraging promises, and before marking this down as another successful treatment, experience has taught us that there is absolutely no way of telling whether these are just empty words or whether there is some level of commitment behind them. The combined expertise of the staff came down on the negative side, and with the assistance of family and friends, Ted entered our long-term (twenty-one-day) treatment.

When Ted was discharged three weeks later, he made similar promises, but this time the staff was more positively persuaded that the denial had been at least broken down to the point that Ted was listening and learning. He has continued his post-discharge counseling and aftercare, as well as attending two or three AA meetings each week. He has been sober for approximately eight months at this writing, and in his own words: "I have to keep telling myself that I am an alcoholic, but every so often I'm really not all that certain. The temptation to have a drink seems to be always present, and when it gets too bad, I call my AA sponsor or go to another AA meeting."

During the final editing stages of this book, I thought about Ted while going over this material and wondered how he was getting along. To my amazement, the very next morning Ted visited our center to announce the second anniversary of his sobriety.

Ted represents an example of what can be called stuporous denial. His original outright denial of having a very severe drinking problem, in spite of its being obvious to all those around him, shows the pharmacological suppression of his thought processes by alcohol. Instead of operating on all eight cylinders, he was lucky if four or five were firing at any one time. Yet he was apparently going through all his usual daily activities, including walking the dog each morning, going to church on Sunday, and, very importantly, going to work each day. As the story unfolded, it turned out he was botching up sales at work practically every day to the point that he was driving customers away. He appeared to be operating at a level of perpetual blackout.

After Ted went through a very severe withdrawal, his mind began to clear up gradually. After almost a week of hospitalization, he was smiling and joking with his fellow patients and the staff. Everyone began to really like Ted. Each day saw a much more happy, enthusiastic, and sharper-thinking person. Each day saw Ted acknowledging his drinking problem in a more open, unembarrassed, and positive way. Each day saw Ted's wife become more understanding of his problem as she progressed through the family counseling sessions. Finally, thirty-three days later, the staff concurred that Ted was ready to go home. Ted himself acknowledged that he was frightened, a marked contrast to his earlier promises, but felt he was as ready as ever to face the challenge of sobriety. With his counselor and AA sponsor, he had worked out a plan to follow. As we shook hands for the final goodbye, the man standing before me looked at least ten years younger than the man I had seen the first day going through withdrawal. He was smiling and saying in a most sincere and positive manner, "Doc, I know I am an alcoholic, and I'm going to give it all I got because I really like the way I feel."

James, on the other hand, showed what can be called stupid denial. He was far from what one would call a stupid person, except when it came to recognizing the effects of his drinking. I first saw James on a medical unit of the hospital after I was asked to consult on the case. He was admitted to the hospital with jaundice (yellowing of the skin) and a large, swollen, tender liver. I did not see him in person until his physician and the resident staff had treated him over a four-day period. James was a sales manager for a large corporation and was, in his own words, doing a good job. He admitted that he drank quite a bit, but said that wining and dining customers was part of his job. He very seldom drank at home because his wife did not approve of drinking.

The reason he had sought medical help was that one day he and his wife were drinking coffee in their kitchen when James glanced out the window and saw what he described as "several men climbing up ladders onto the roof of my neighbor's house." He asked his wife, "What are the Joneses having done to their roof?" She looked out the window, saw no one, and said jokingly, "You must be seeing things." But James insisted that there were men climbing a ladder and he counted them: "one, two, three, four..." Now his wife became frightened and together they decided that James had better see his doctor. The next thing he knew, he was in the hospital being told that his liver had been badly damaged and he had to stop drinking if he wanted to live. Apparently, that's all James and his wife had to hear, because he quickly sought out our alcohol treatment program. Rather than coming begrudgingly, he became a little upset that we weren't moving the transfer along faster. All he needed to hear was that alcohol was hurting his body. Yes, he had heard about how too much drinking could hurt your liver, but he seemed to feel it happened to the other guy and couldn't happen to him: "I guess I just didn't appreciate how much I was drinking and that alcohol could cause this type of damage. Boy, was I *stupid*!"

James entered our treatment program. Eating well, resting, not drinking and time saw his liver began to return to a normal, functional state. He participated actively in all the group therapy sessions, lectures, and educational movies, attended "off-campus" AA meetings two to three times per week, and worked well with his wife and daughter in family counseling sessions. He was discharged twenty-eight days later looking and feeling fine; his parting words to me were, "Doc, I learned the most important lesson of my life!"

Finally, there is what can be called secretive denial. This is done by the person who knows in his heart that he has a drinking problem, but doesn't want to tell anyone about it, especially himself. He usually gets angry if anyone brings up the subject, yet he keeps telling himself that he really should cut down. People comment on occasion, "Boy, did you notice him last night, he was really putting them away!" The next day he may even apologize to his host and hostess for making a fool of himself. The reassuring reply he usually gets is, "Oh, we understand, we all have to let loose once in a while."

The thought of going to an AA meeting has passed

through his mind, but it's too risky ("I might meet someone I know"). He goes to his physician for a checkup, in the course of which he may mention: "I have a friend who's really drinking heavily and I'm beginning to worry about him. Is there anyone he can talk to about his drinking?" As is so often the case, the friend and the person asking the concerned questions are one and the same. Eventually, the person in secretive denial gets into trouble because of his drinking. Most likely this will be a DWI. He appears in court acknowledging that he had been drinking, but saying he really doesn't feel he has a problem. The person in secretive denial will get into trouble again and again unless there is some sort of intervention to get him into a treatment program. If left untreated, he will probably progress into a state of stuporous denial, wherein the anesthetic effects of alcohol perpetually cloud his awareness of the problem.

This type of denial is not confined to the disease of alcoholism. I feel it is characteristic of all of us. Some would have us believe that all denial stems from the ultimate denial we live with all our lives—that in spite of anything and everything we do in life we will some day die. But the whole thrust of our culture and society is to prolong life as much as possible. Youth expresses itself with optimism and looks to the seemingly endless future. Aging causes changes in this perspective. While some cling to the appearance of youth and deny the inevitable, others, accepting the inevitable, enjoy life one day at a time. Still others sit back and patiently await the inevitable. The Mayan culture of several thousand years ago viewed "returning to the Gods" as a desirable goal, and human sacrifices were intended to hasten the realization of this opportunity. (The one to be sacrificed was amply drugged so as not to contradict the wisdom of this belief before the final act.)

Physicians are particularly prone to this type of secretive denial. They may experience a certain discomfort or pain in some part of the body. They engage in self-diagnosis, don't like what they conclude (cancer, heart disease, ulcer), and, in all too many instances, ignore the problem. They continue ignoring or denying the problem to the point where the pain is unbearable or they can't perform their work, and only then will they seek help. Even at this point, they try to keep it a secret from their friends and colleagues. Unfortunately, there are times when they never make it to the point of seeking help.

Starting almost on the first day of medical school, we were urged by one professor not to treat members of our families because we might lose our sense of objectivity. We might not see things we didn't want to see in a loved one or deny what we saw because we didn't want to see anything that suggested a serious medical problem. Above all, we were told not to treat ourselves. A physician who treats himself has "A fool for a patient, and a bigger fool for a doctor."

Denial is characteristic of human behavior and can occur within all of us under certain circumstances. But how do we deal with the denial of the alcoholic? How do we convince someone that he needs help? Members of the alcoholic's family may deal with the problem by engaging in their own denial and just learn to live with it. In so doing, they become enablers. However, at some point, the problem becomes impossible to ignore, because alcoholism will continue to get worse until some form of treatment, or death, intervenes. Unfortunately, the latter resolution prevails all too frequently.

Thousands of people enter alcoholism treatment programs in the United States every year. Perhaps we can learn something from them. You may recall that earlier we said the treatment for alcoholism is education, persuasion, and coercion. It is coercion that brings most people to an alcohol treatment center to be admitted on a voluntary basis. And self-admission to an alcohol treatment center can be the first step in the process of breaking down the shell of denial. Patients voluntarily present themselves to our treatment center for one of five reasons:

1) Self-Coercion. "I'm sick of being sick," or "I can't stand to look at myself in the mirror each morning any more, I'm such a mess," or "I can't stand living like this any more, my life isn't going anyplace."

2) Family Coercion. "My wife took the kids and left me last week because of my drinking," or "I just couldn't stand to see my daughter cry when I came home drunk again," or "They all ganged up on me at dinner last night. Anything to keep the peace in the family!" or "My wife and daughter started going to Al-Anon several weeks ago. I couldn't believe it!"

3) Employer Coercion. "You are a great worker when you are here—you have more aunts and uncles dying whose funeral you must attend than anyone I have ever known. Either get treatment or look for another job." Or, "Ted, this is the third big sale you botched up because of your drinking. Why don't you get some help? Otherwise I don't know if I can convince the home office we shouldn't let you go."

4) *Legal Coercion.* "The court ordered me into treatment after my thirty-day jail sentence when I got my third DWI," or "My lawyer said it would look good when I went to court on the disorderly conduct charge."

5) *Physician Coercion.* Five years ago I never heard a patient say, "My doctor said I better get treatment if I wanted to live." Now I am hearing this theme from an increasing number of patients presenting themselves for admission. I hope this will continue to increase as the medical community gains an even greater appreciation of the disease concept of alcoholism.

But what about the person with a drinking problem who may admit to drinking too much once in a while but will hear no talk about entering a treatment program? "First of all I don't need it, besides, it costs a lot of money." The technique that can be used most successfully is called intervention. The basic element of the technique is to bring together all of the significant people in the life of the intended patient and have each one, in a surprise-type group setting, bombard the subject with instances like the following related to his or her behavior during specific drinking episodes:

"Dad, do you remember the time you staggered out of the bedroom and urinated on the kitchen floor while my friends and I were doing our homework?"

"Dad, you really embarrassed me in front of all my classmates when you came to my graduation drunk."

"Jim, it really hurt when after all these years of our close friendship you started calling me all those four-letter words when you were drunk."

"Jim, do you remember the Sunday I had to help you out of church because you were so drunk you interrupted the sermon?"

"Jim, do you remember that at the last board of directors' meeting you started snoring because you had too many drinks for lunch?"

I estimate that as often as 95 percent of the time, the individual will voluntarily admit him or herself to a treatment center as a result. A note of caution—this approach can backfire very seriously if not done properly, and I highly recommend that a professional person with expertise in this field be in charge of the whole process. This is by no means a home-remedy type of treatment!

Denial is part of the disease process. It can and has to be dealt with for the sake of the patient and those around him or her. There are people who can help. Don't give up, for everyone's sake!

TEN

Who Should Be Treated and How?

What is the treatment for alcoholism? First, I would like to give you the definition upon which our program at St. Thomas Medical Center is based:

Alcoholism is an incurable disease that starts at the time of diagnosis [for practical considerations only] and ends at the time of death. However, this interim period between the two points can be extended into a normal, happy and productive life if one accepts and practices the necessity for treatment for the rest of his or her life.

We are saying that alcoholism cannot be cured but rather has to be "managed." This is true of essentially all chronic diseases. We do not cure diabetes mellitus, but by following a certain diet and/or injecting an appropriate amount of insulin each day, we can maintain a normal blood sugar level like that of a nondiabetic. Similarly, hypertension is managed by regulating salt intake and, if necessary, taking prescribed medications daily. In most people this will result in a normal blood pressure. But what do we offer the alcoholic for his or her disease? Simply stated, it's "Don't drink alcohol!" This is the bottom line of any treatment. There are no pills or shots in the arm that we can offer. Education, persuasion, and coercion are the only tools we have to combat this disease.

The role of coercion is most important in getting the patient exposed to the other two components of treatment, and when the patient presents himself or herself to our center on a voluntary basis, this component has already been accomplished. All the patients admitted to our center are there because of one of the five forms of coercion, coming from the self, family, employer, court, or doctor. Just as a patient voluntarily admits himself or herself to an alcoholism treatment unit, he or she can also leave at any time— simply walk out or leave AMA (against medical advice). None of our patients can be forced to stay against his will.

Treating the Body

Once in the door, what happens next? First a nurse interviews the patient. Questions focus on general health: any illnesses; is he or she taking any medications, and if so, the name of the drug, the dose, and how often; any specific pains or complaints; an alcohol intake history—"What do you usually drink? How much do you drink? When did you have your last drink?" and so forth. Then a laboratory technician takes blood samples to determine the blood alcohol level and the presence of any other drugs, liver function tests, and a blood cell count. Other tests include a urinalysis, an electrocardiogram, and a chest X-ray. Most of the tests are done routinely for any patient admitted to a hospital. All of these tests are done within the first hour or so of admission to our unit.

What happens next depends on the clinical state of the patient. If the patient is not severely intoxicated, or showing signs of acute withdrawal, then he is taken to his room and begins to settle into the routine of the center. By this time the patient's blood alcohol level is reported from the laboratory and, following the physician's standing orders, the nursing staff will usually start medicating the patient with Librium. By way of chemical pathways not completely understood, the Librium counteracts the physiological changes occurring in the body when the cells are deprived of alcohol. The dose of Librium is usually reduced over the next four days as the signs and symptoms of withdrawal lessen. If the patient is intoxicated or showing signs of severe withdrawal, particularly tremors or hallucinations, he is usually put to bed and observed very closely—blood pressure, pulse, respiration, and body temperature—and the Librium is given more frequently by the nurse.

Soon the physician in charge will carry out a complete history and physical examination. Based on this exam and the laboratory findings, the physician will assess the patient's overall state of health. If underlying diseases or complications are diagnosed, the physician will start the appropriate treatment, including calling in specialists if necessary: cardiologists for heart problems; a gastroenterologist when there is significant injury to the liver, stomach, or intestinal tract (such as ulcers); or a urologist when there is a urinary tract problem or (in males) a prostate problem. The hematologist is called if the patient is anemic (too few red blood cells or too many white blood cells, suggesting some type of injury to the bone marrow). The neurologist consults on any problem with the nervous system, such as severe numbness and tingling in the arms and/or legs. The dermatologist will treat any serious rash or skin disorder, and so on throughout the entire body and range of medical practice. This thorough medical assessment is in keeping with the original tenets of AA; that is, the need to treat the body, the mind, and the soul, or in modern-day medical thinking, the whole person (holistic medicine). Treating the body is extremely important, not only in the sense of alleviating pain and suffering, but in terms of its impact on one's drinking behavior.

I've heard it countless times: "Doc, the only thing that helps the pain is alcohol!" Keith is a retired salesman who had a long-standing history of a degenerative bone disease of the spine. He had been in and out of hospitals numerous times with no successful treatment or relief from the pain. As he told me, "Doc, the easiest way for me to deal with this pain is to get drunk." Working closely with orthopedists (bone doctors) and rheumatologists (joint doctors) we worked out a treatment plan for Keith. By continuing his medications and becoming very active in AA, Keith has dealt with his medical problem without alcohol for almost two years at this writing.

Gerry was fifty-five years old when he was admitted to our unit, but he looked at least seventy-five. He was a physical wreck. He had very severe emphysema, or chronic obstructive pulmonary disease (COPD). He could hardly get himself from his room to the dining area without resting every few steps, yet he was always puffing on a cigarette. Several physicians had literally given up on him. His alcohol problem only made matters worse and seemed to complicate his breathing problem. But I want to tell you something else about Gerry. Gerry never smiled. One might say that with his damaged lungs and breathing problems, what would you expect? However, Gerry also had two big lumps on his face, one on each cheek. One was the size of a plum and the other the size of a cherry. Frankly, they made Gerry look ugly and attracted stares from everyone.

When I talked to Gerry about having these lumps removed, his answer was: "I've had these for years." I was pretty insistent that I thought they should be removed. I told him he would feel better about himself, especially when he looked in the mirror. He confessed that he was truly embarrassed and felt intensely uncomfortable about the lumps, but never had the courage to have them removed. None of his physicians had ever suggested it either. He told me a story of how he was riding on a city bus one day and two teenagers got on and started towards the rear of the bus. When they passed Gerry, they stopped and stared and made a comment like, "Ugh, gross!" gesturing with their hands "stay away from me." Gerry said he felt so bad he got off the bus immediately, five stops too soon, and felt like crying. Anyway, we had a surgeon remove the two lumps. Although he still has breathing problems, his face looks so much better, and, more importantly, Gerry actually smiles when he comes back to the center for a visit.

Treating the Mind

Treating the mind does not necessarily mean psychiatric intervention. As pointed out earlier, approximately three out of ten of our patients are seen by psychiatrists and have been treated for a psychiatric disorder. But that's not the kind of treating the mind I'm talking about here. What I mean is the education and persuasion referred to earlier. Our education and persuasion program include lectures, movies, group therapy sessions, individual counseling, visits with AA members, and AA meetings where an invited member gives a lead, that is, tells the story of his or her life with alcohol and how they were able to turn it around. Our lectures and classes cover topics like how to deal with stress in your life, relaxation therapy, occupational therapy, supervised art classes, lectures on nutrition, and supervised physical activity. One activity, called Honesty Group, soon becomes a favorite of the patients. This is a closed session where only the patients and the nurse/counselor are present; the basic ground rule is that nothing said in the group is repeated outside the session. Initially, new patients feel some discomfort in discussing any very personal aspect of their lives, but those who have been in the unit longer provide the encouragement and support to "tell it like it is." These types of activities tend to give the patients a new basis on which to start looking at themselves from a positive perspective rather than a negative one. They report: "Doc, I have learned so much about myself that I never knew," or "I have been able to say things that I have been keeping inside for years. It feels like someone has taken a big rock off of my back."

Treating the Soul

Treating the soul can become rather controversial, depending upon one's religious or spiritual persuasions. However, I have had only one patient walk out because he couldn't handle the spiritual aspects of the program, particularly reciting the Serenity Prayer each day:

> *God, grant me the serenity*
> *To accept the things I cannot change,*
> *Courage to change the things I can,*
> *And wisdom to know the difference.*

There are no specific or prescribed rules to the spiritual component; rather, we take an individual approach, allotting time for meditation upon arising in the morning and before retiring for the evening. As one of AA's 12 Steps states—"To turn our lives over to the care of God as we understand him."

I have described the treatment plan followed by Ignatia Hall, but it is representative of the type of program followed in many alcohol treatment facilities:

1) One must first deal with the acute withdrawal signs and symptoms as the patient experiences the effects of abstinence from alcohol, if they have become physically dependent.

2) A medical assessment is made and any underlying diseases or complications must be diagnosed and treated.

3) Any acute psychiatric problems must be diagnosed and treatment started.

4) Participation in the educational and psychosocial phases of the program are started as soon after admission as possible, depending on the physical status of the patient, while the pains associated with alcohol are still fresh in the patient's mind.

5) A social service assessment is carried out to address the patient's home situation.
6) An interdisciplinary team helps the patient work out a discharge plan, including aftercare, medical appointments, and attending AA meetings.
7) The patient is discharged.

How long does this treatment program take? The original treatment program developed by Dr. Bob (Robert H. Smith, M.D.), one of the co-founders of AA, and Sister Ignatia was six days. We must remember that back in 1939 relatively little was known about the sequence of events that occurred when coming off alcohol. I'm sure six days was consistent with the notion of getting the patient back to work as soon as possible as part of the therapy. It might also have been the maximum length of time a patient could stomach Dr. Bob's Karo syrup, sauerkraut, and tomato juice diet. This six-day program became a tradition that Ignatia Hall followed until 1982.

In the 1950s a new twenty-eight-day treatment program model came out of several centers in the United States and Canada. The new model caught on, and soon twenty-eight-day programs began to appear throughout the United States. Most health insurance companies accepted the rationale of the twenty-eight-day program and agreed to pay benefits for up to that length of time. When I entered the alcoholism field, all I heard about was the twenty-eight-day program. Frankly, I was puzzled, because I knew of no other disease in medicine where one could predict that the treatment would take exactly twenty-eight days for each and every patient. It was quickly pointed out to me that the twenty-eight-day program had become the standard model *because this was the amount of hospital days that insurance companies would cover for payment.*

Insurance companies usually offer different types of coverage for inpatient and outpatient treatment. Inpatient can refer to anything from a medical unit of a hospital to a fancy resort-type setting, as long as one is there on a full-time basis. Outpatient programs are any activities where the patient goes to the hospital or treatment center, but returns home, each night, or carries on a normal work week. Today there are a variety of types of treatment programs and philosophic approaches, including:

1) Detox programs.   These inpatient programs are designed to treat the patient during the acute phase of withdrawal from alcohol. Most are three to four days long and pay relatively little time and attention to the educational and behavioral aspects of treatment.

2) Acute treatment programs.   These are usually seven to eight days in duration in an inpatient setting in a hospital. The program not only deals with the detoxification phase, but starts the patient on the road to recovery. Most acute programs focus on the patient's attitude, behavior, and other psychosocial aspects of treatment as well as dealing with any physical complications.

3) Modified acute treatment programs.   Usually about fourteen days in duration, these inpatient programs deal with the detoxification phase and extend the rehabilitative phase of treatment.

4) Extended care treatment programs. Most are twenty-eight days in an inpatient setting such as a hospital or residence hall. Usually, the patient has already been detoxed, either in a separate setting or perhaps another facility entirely. The program concentrates on counseling and/or behavior modification-type activities.

5) Long-term treatment programs. Anywhere from one to six months in duration, usually in a residential setting with a minimum of medical resources, long-term programs try to effect long-lasting behavioral changes. They generally emphasize things like getting to know yourself better and trying to build on those things you like and change the things you don't like about yourself.

6) Aftercare outpatient treatment. Most inpatient programs have an aftercare treatment program following discharge. These may be individual or group counseling sessions. Usually, visits are once a week, and there is no prescribed period of time for the treatment. Patient and counselors often mutually agree on the duration.

7) Outpatient treatment. Patients who don't require hospitalization may have individual counseling in a professional's office once or twice a week, attend a structured series of classes, or undergo some other form of treatment. Again, the focus is on education, counseling, and behavioral change. Recently, there has been talk in our community about having physicians do outpatient detox treatment in their offices. Although I'm certain this could be done with selected patients, as a general rule, I believe detoxification should be done in a medical setting with all necessary medical resources immediately available, because this can be a potentially life-threatening situation.

8) *Intensive outpatient day treatment programs.*   Although essentially outpatient programs, the patient will spend the whole day, usually six to eight hours, in the professional institutional setting. These programs are designed to provide all the behavioral and training techniques exactly as if the patient were in an inpatient treatment program. The difference is that the patient sleeps in his or her own bed at home at night.

9) *Halfway house.*   This is an attempt to provide a home away from home sort of setting, usually during the transition from a treatment center to the mainstream of everyday life. These are usually residential houses where a group of recovering alcoholics live, going to work each day and engaging in other everyday activities. Supervision is usually minimal, with perhaps a live-in manager, and there is usually a minimum of formal and structured treatment activities.

10) *Employee Assistance Programs (EAPs).*   These are either in-house or contracted services for employees of a given company. The EAP usually provides counseling not only for alcohol problems, but for drug abuse, or any type of psychological problem that could interfere with the employee's efficiency at work or satisfaction with his or her job.

11) *Alcoholics Anonymous.*   AA is a unique self-help fellowship. It is loosely, but very effectively, organized as a

nonprofit organization for recovering alcoholics. Each affili-
ated AA group meets at a designated place and time on a
regular basis, usually once a week. The groups define themselves as either closed or open meeting. The former is
restricted to recovering alcoholics, and the latter is open to
anyone who is interested in the problem of alcoholism. AA
meetings are held throughout the world and at just about
any day or time of the week, depending on the size of the
city or town. It is said that in New York City, there is an
AA meeting being held every hour of a twenty-four-hour
day, seven days a week. In my judgement, there is a certain
beauty inherent in the simplicity of these meetings. This
follows one of the co-founder's admonitions, made here in
Akron just over fifty years ago, to "Keep it simple!" The
meeting traditionally starts with a welcome by a chairperson:
"Hi, my name is _____ and I am an alcoholic." The audience
responds in unison, "Hi, _____." Then a preselected person
gives the lead—tells his or her story about the struggle with
alcohol. Sometimes one of the Twelve Steps or Twelve Tradi-
tions is discussed in depth. Audience participation follows,
with comments from members who express their thanks and
gratitude for the opportunity to hear the lead and how it
affected them personally. At the end, the group will usually
hold hands and say in unison the Lord's Prayer or the
Serenity Prayer, a most thrilling and inspirational experience
for a nonmember. Then comes a period of socializing with
coffee (more recently, juice has been added because caffeine
is a drug, too) and other refreshments. Then everyone
returns to his everyday life challenges, in my judgement,
better prepared to face them.

12) Al-Anon.   An offshoot of AA made up of the family members of alcoholics, Al-Anon groups welcome anyone whose life has been influenced by alcoholism. Al-Anon groups meet at regular times with essentially the same format as an AA meeting, except that the lead is sometimes a discussion panel made up of family members, relatives, or friends of alcoholics. The group's purpose is to better understand the problem of alcoholism and learn effective ways to cope with the problems it entails.

More and more professional attention is being focused on the family of the alcoholic. New information demonstrates that a condition called codependency usually exists in an alcoholic's family. The alcoholic's significant others (family, friends, etc.) are codependent when their behavior feeds or reinforces the alcoholic's problems. Codependent people have had to develop maladaptive behavior in order to co-exist with the alcoholic. We sometimes label this situation enabling, and the person involved, an enabler. The concept of codependency recognizes that the enablers create their own problems in the complex interactions of adjusting to or coping with an alcoholic's behavior. Increasing recognition of codependency has led some to consider it a separate and distinct disease and to develop the field of Family Systems Therapy.

13) Alateen.   Alateen is a self-help group specifically for teenagers whose parent or parents are alcoholics. Alateen gives the children of alcoholics a chance to share their feelings and gain a better understanding of what is happening in their lives.

14) Adult Children of Alcoholics (ACA or ACOA). More recently, adults have been discovering that they have certain emotional scars from growing up in an alcoholic home. There are separate groups, either independent or under the umbrella of Al-Anon, that address the special problems of adult children of alcoholics, some of whom may be recovering alcoholics themselves.

15) Psychiatric Treatment. I feel something should be said about the role of psychiatry in the treatment of alcoholism. The reason for my hesitation about including this topic is that many alcoholics I have known, particularly recovering alcoholics, are very skeptical about the help a psychiatrist has to offer, "I am an alcoholic, but I am not a *crazy* alcoholic." At least in this part of the country, the skepticism comes from a difference of opinion during the early days of founding AA. As some of the old-timers in AA describe the situation then, psychiatrists were focusing on the possible "causes" of the disease, such as lack of affection in early childhood, while the alcoholics were looking for someone to help them deal with their immediate pain and disease process.

Another factor that widened the gap has been the real or perceived promiscuous use of antipsychotic, antidepressant, and antianxiety medications (commonly called mood-altering drugs) by psychiatrists. The alcoholic was trying to get his or her mind clear from the effects of alcohol and it seemed to many that the psychiatrist was clouding it up again with a variety of drugs, some of them addictive. I will always remember hearing at one AA meeting, "Valium is nothing but dehydrated gin!"

The irony of this seeming conflict is that in the early days

of AA, Bill W. conferred with one of the foremost psychiatrists of his day, Karl Jung. Bill W. accepted the fact that in
some instances, psychiatric involvement was absolutely essential in the treatment of an alcoholic. He wrote that: *"It is
the business of psychiatry to get behind our excuses [for
drinking] and to find deeper causes for our conduct. We
ought to look with the deepest respect, interest, and profit
upon the findings of psychiatry."*

Fortunately, this gap in thinking has narrowed in recent
times as both groups have gained a better understanding of
the disease. We have learned to question whether bizarre or
inappropriate behavior is due to the effects of alcohol alone,
or stems from superimposing alcohol upon a pre-existing
psychiatric disorder—a dual disease syndrome. The dual
disease diagnosis is becoming more and more readily accepted, and many of the barriers that were erected to keep the
psychiatrist and his or her bag full of mood-altering drugs
away from the alcoholic are gradually being broken down.
As mentioned earlier, neither animals nor humans will self-
administer or develop an addiction to most drugs like aspirin, digitalis, or insulin, and even those that act on the brain
like haloperidol, lithium, or antidepressants.

The practical dilemma faced by professionals in an alcohol
treatment center is what one does with an intoxicated person
who is doing crazy things, including threatening to jump off
a bridge. No one will deny that alcohol can make you do
and say crazy things, and at times it is next to impossible
even for a psychiatrist to determine whether alcohol is the
cause of the behavior or if there is an underlying mental
illness. In our own treatment program there is an excellent
working relationship with the psychiatry department. Pa-

tients who are admitted to the psychiatry unit for severe emotional problems, including suicidal thoughts, are readily transferred to the alcohol treatment center when they become clinically stable and it appears that their behavior was influenced more by alcohol. Similarly, patients who manifest significant emotional problems in the alcohol treatment center are seen by the psychiatrist, who can begin treatment with the appropriate medication if indicated, as well as follow the patient throughout the hospital stay and after discharge.

Only rarely have we found it necessary to transfer a patient from the alcohol to the psychiatric unit, because ours is an open unit, and a patient can leave or walk out AMA at any time. The psychiatric unit is a closed unit or locked ward, which permits confinement of the patient for his or her self-protection, and in some instances, for the protection of others. I mention this point because a significant number of our patients during the early withdrawal phases describe feelings of fear that they are "losing it." Their greatest fear, which adds to the problem, is that we are going to take them through the door and put them in the looney bin or the crazy ward. With the help of our psychiatrist, we can reassure them in most instances that they are not crazy, but that the effects of the alcohol make them feel crazy. This insistence on the use of the word crazy reflects their attitude toward psychiatry and psychiatrists, a view that is widespread among the public. I see a crying need for more public awareness and education about mental illness and its relationship to the disease of alcoholism.

16) A good diet, rest, no alcohol, and time.   In addition to our emphasis on education and persuasion, there is a significant healing process going on in the body that we sometimes overlook or ignore. Just the simple routine of eating a nutritionally sound diet on a regular schedule, getting regularly scheduled rest—not going several days without sleep and trying to catch up on the weekend—and, of course, staying away from alcohol, has an amazing healing action on the body that has been physically abused by alcohol.

Let me tell you about Dick. At age fifty-eight he was admitted to a medical floor of the hospital with a diagnosis of bleeding ulcers. I was called in to consult after the bleeding was controlled and his behavior indicated an alcohol problem. When I saw Dick for the first time, I was somewhat taken aback because he was literally a physical wreck. He was thin, pale, toothless, and the need for a shave and a haircut made him look twenty years older. To make matters worse, he had been tied down to his bed with restraints to keep him from falling out of bed or from wandering down the halls and possibly hurting himself if he fell. He was also hard of hearing, if not deaf, and he had lost his hearing aid before he came to the hospital. Talking to him brought only a blank stare, although there were times when I thought certain facial expressions hinted that he could hear what he wanted to hear. I know he heard me when I suggested he be transferred to the alcoholism treatment unit because he kept saying "No, no, no!" each time I brought it up. But further discussion convinced him to enter the program—at least he didn't resist when we wheeled him over to the unit in a wheelchair. The staff had mixed feelings about Dick. "If he can't hear, how can he participate in the group sessions?" or "He is so physically debilitated and weak he will fall asleep through all the program activities." All were legitimate concerns.

At first, Dick was very withdrawn and would just sit in the group sessions staring straight ahead and not saying a word. During the movies he would always fall asleep until his snoring became annoying. At mealtimes he would more or less just play with his food. The staff then decided that this man needed some extra T.L.C. First we worked on his appearance, arranging a haircut and convincing him to shave off the beard he was growing. Then we arranged for social services to get him a new hearing aid. We then focused on feeding him. Soon he was showing up for all three meals on his own. Instead of shuffling down the hall, he was walking rather briskly. He started going to sleep at 10:50 P.M. and slept until 7:30 A.M. Soon he was smiling. However, his hearing was less than optimal, even with a hearing aid. The other patients began to be more friendly with him and they nicknamed him Pops. Soon he took the initiative in starting conversations with the staff and other patients. He started to gain weight and his skin color began to return to normal. He began to look like a man in his fifties rather than his seventies. One had the impression that you could almost see him gain new strength each day. All of this happened in the course of sixteen days, and the only medication he received during that time was a daily vitamin tablet.

Then a twenty-six-year-old man was admitted to the unit, and several days later he asked to speak to me. When I sat down with him, he seemed as excited as a little boy who had just seen Santa Claus for the first time. The conversation went something like this:

"Do you know who that old man is [describing Dick]?"

"No, not really, other than that he was really sick when he came to the hospital."

"That man is a master mechanic and the best engine mechanic in northeastern Ohio. He has made some of the fastest racing cars ever, but no one has seen him in the past four or five years. Wow, wait until I tell my friends about this."

Dick was discharged twenty-one days after admission and was literally a new man. All his laboratory tests were reported as normal; he was much more alert, more talkative, and with a wonderful sense of humor. We will never know how much we taught him about behavior modification or how to stay sober. When he was saying his goodbyes, it was one of those moments in medicine when you have the feeling that there is absolutely no question in your mind that it's all worth it in spite of everything.

Through the grapevine, we learned that Dick was back working on cars. About six months after his discharge, he surprised us all when he visited us in the unit accompanied by a woman about half his age whom he introduced as his girlfriend.

The point to be made is that in spite of the arguments that much of alcoholism treatment can be carried out in an outpatient setting rather than in an expensive hospital room, or even in a less expensive intermediate care facility, there is something to be argued in favor of placing a patient in a structured environment for an extended period. There, the healing process has a chance to take place in his or her body with little chance of a relapse. The treatment plan that works best is good diet, rest, no alcohol, and time.

17) Antabuse Treatment. For the sake of completeness, I should say something about Antabuse (Disulfiram). Many years ago, factory workers who worked with certain sulfur-containing solvents noticed that when they drank a glass of beer during lunch or immediately after work, they experienced a flushed or flushing sensation in the head and neck, an increased heart rate, sweating, difficulty in breathing, and some nausea, plus a headache. By process of elimination, they solved the problem by not drinking beer. Through serendipity (capitalizing on a chance happening or observation) this led to encapsulating a chemical relative of the sulfur-containing compound and introducing it as Antabuse, as a treatment regimen for alcoholism.

Basically, the Antabuse blocks the chemical reaction that breaks down the acetaldehyde produced from the metabolism of alcohol. Because its breakdown is blocked, acetaldehyde accumulates in the blood. As we noted earlier, it is the accumulation of acetaldehyde after a heavy bout of drinking that causes the so-called hangover. Thus, people taking Antabuse set themselves up for an immediate hangover if they drink. The rationale for its use is to develop an aversion to alcohol, knowing that it will make you sick immediately if you are on Antabuse. But does this work?

Unfortunately, many patients look to Antabuse as a cure for their disease, but soon find this is not the case. The people who are unsuccessful with Antabuse are those who failed to understand that the basic drive to drink is still present, and the role of Antabuse is to reinforce the behavior modification in changing their lifestyle patterns. We view the use of Antabuse as an intermediate step in coming to the point of self-controlled abstinence.

Approximately 1 percent of our patients are discharged on Antabuse and, to date, their relapse rate is about the same as that for those not on Antabuse. There is no question in my mind that there is a time and place for Antabuse in the treatment of alcoholism, but there is a lot more involved than giving the patient a prescription for some pills so that everything will be fine. One must continue to work on his or her sobriety. Antabuse can provide temporary assistance, but it will not solve the problem.

18) *Controlled drinking.* "John, you must understand this, listen very carefully: you have injured your body and you can never drink again!" With few exceptions, this is part of the final discussion I have with each patient before discharge. The response varies, but most patients respond, "Oh, don't worry, Doc, I'll never drink again," or "You will never see me again as a patient." I believe that the majority of these patients really mean what they say, but I always remind them of something I was told over and over again as a medical student: "Never say 'never' in medicine." I emphasize to each patient that he or she is very vulnerable to starting to drink again. "Remember, you are just one drink away from being a drunk! Don't take that first drink!" and the AA advice, "Don't think about whether you will ever drink again, just don't drink today. One Day At A Time." At Ignatia Hall we adhere strictly to the original philosophy of AA since its founding over fifty years ago: that the only "cure" for alcoholism is abstinence.

About twenty-five years ago it was suggested for the first time, based upon coincidental observations and impressions, that an alcoholic could return to normal or controlled drinking after treatment. Since then, two studies, one called the Rand Report and another written by two behavioral psychologists, have supported the idea that it was possible for alcoholics to return to normal drinking behavior. These studies received a great deal of attention in the media and stirred up a hornet's nest of controversy. This kind of thinking flew in the face of the long-standing treatment philosophy of total abstinence.

These studies have been extensively criticized, as might be anticipated given the controversial nature of the findings. They have been attacked for poor scientific design, poor methodological technique, absence of clinical expertise and judgement—even accusations of scientific fraud. On the other hand, there have been a few reports that supported the conclusions of these studies.

The treatment philosophy of Ignatia Hall, since its founding in 1939, has been *abstinence*. Approximately half of our patients who relapse and are readmitted describe how they tried some form of controlled drinking and found that soon they were back to progressive loss-of-control drinking.

Jean and her husband John were both recovering alcoholics. She had twelve months of sobriety and he had eighteen months when, influenced by media coverage of controlled drinking, they planned in a careful and detailed manner to start a controlled drinking program on John's fiftieth birthday. In three months, Jean was drinking progressively more heavily with total lack of control. When she was admitted, she told us how John was still practicing controlled drinking. However, two and a half months later John was seeking help because he had lost control.

Will this happen in every case of controlled drinking? I

don't know. As I have said time and time again, the treatment for this disease of alcoholism has to be individualized to account for tremendous variations in people and their practices. The data is not yet available to predict with absolute certainty the success or failure of someone going through a treatment program. However, I would consider it an act of malpractice to even suggest to one of our patients that they may be able to drink again through controlled drinking. Abstinence is still the order of the day for anyone discharged from our program.

19) "Successful" or "unsuccessful" treatment. When people learn that I treat alcoholics, the question they ask most often is "How successful are you in your treatment?" There is always the expectation in medicine that we the physicians cure disease, and, accordingly, have either been successful or have failed. Closer scrutiny reveals that we actually attempt to manage or control the disease to alleviate pain and suffering. We never cure it. But I always feel that the intent of the question is to find out whether or not the patients really stop drinking, which is believed to be the cure for the disease.

Sister Ignatia often said before her retirement in 1951 and mentioned in her writings afterward that about 60 to 65 percent of the patients who left Ignatia Hall stayed on the wagon following discharge, and the others fell off the wagon within one year. Interestingly, this is about the same figure (67 percent) that is currently considered the standard of success for all alcohol treatment centers. Recently, these figures have been challenged, because there are indications that the numbers have been inflated by some treatment centers as part of a marketing program to attract new patients—the ones who can pay, of course.

The whole question of determining the rate of successful outcomes is much more complex than is sometimes appreciated. The very question of what constitutes a successful outcome brings a variety of answers, from maintaining sobriety for X amount of time to reflections about the quality of life after treatment. There is also the question of follow-up statistics after discharge. In an area like ours, where a large corporation can decide to move to another area of the country, disrupting whole neighborhoods, many patients can be lost for the purpose of follow-up studies.

One very important factor is the socioeconomic class of people admitted to a treatment center. It has been found that programs that cater to upper-middle-class individuals—those with a stable family life, a steady job, and more to lose, so to speak—have a higher success rate than those centers which serve primarily members of lower socioeconomic classes.

Still another complicating factor is the increasing number of new alcohol treatment centers being opened across the nation. Estimates range from 7,000 to 8,000 new treatment programs during a five-year period (1983–1988), a 65 percent increase. However, recent changes in health insurance policies limiting coverage for alcoholism treatment, especially in an in-patient setting, has seen the number of treatment centers decrease significantly, particularly the private or for-profit facilities. Nevertheless, several treatment centers usually remain within a certain region, which permits patients to go treatment-center hopping.

Because of federal regulations intended to protect the

patient's confidentiality, it is very difficult to validate a given patient's history of previous treatment. Many times we learn this information only when the patient's insurance company writes to tell us they will not pay for a patient's hospital stay because this is his or her tenth or eleventh or whatever treatment. In our own center, close to 55 percent of the patients admitted say they have previously been admitted to our or other alcohol treatment programs. Perhaps some day it will be possible for all treatment centers to compare notes and still maintain confidentiality, as has long been done with Cancer Registries to obtain statistics on the prevalence of cancer in different states and countries. Then it would be possible to talk about success rates with more precision and confidence.

Perhaps sobriety is not the best indication of success. All chronic diseases left untreated will eventually result in death, but with proper treatment and management the life that is prolonged can have more or less quality. An important question we could ask is whether treated patients live longer than untreated patients, just as we talk of five-year and ten-year survival rates to judge the effectiveness of cancer treatment programs.

At present, our follow-up statistics are focusing more on the number of patients who are repeat admissions. During a twelve-month period in 1985–1986, the percentage of repeat admissions at our center was 41 percent, whereas for a twelve-month period in 1980–1981, the percent of repeat admissions was closer to 60 percent. Whether we are, therefore, being more successful, or whether these figures only reflect the complicating factors noted earlier, only time and further analysis will tell.

In spite of the numerous kinds of alcohol treatment programs and types of approaches, several basic elements are common to their spectrum of treatment: 1) a detoxification component, 2) a medical assessment and treatment component, 3) a counseling and/or behavior modification component, either as inpatient or outpatient, and 4) an aftercare or follow-up component. Most of the programs differ in their approach to the third component of the program. They will use one-on-one counseling, group therapy, behavior modification, relaxation therapy, stress management therapy, teaching coping skills, AA meetings and spiritual meditations, and any of a variety of techniques.

But above all, the patient must be impressed with the fact that his or her treatment program after discharge is mostly a first step in a lifelong treatment program. AA members use the expression "working my program" to describe their lifelong effort. And for most recovering alcoholics, working their program will mean attending AA meetings regularly. It has been reported in recent years that approximately 58 percent of those entering the AA fellowship were abstaining after one year. But those who had been in the fellowship more than five years had a 92 percent chance of being sober for another year. Although these figures could be challenged because of the anonymity issue in collecting these kinds of statistics, few would not agree that AA works.

I have to tell you about Joe, one of our daily visitors to the center. He sits in one of the chairs in the visitors' section we keep for AA members, drinking a cup of coffee (without cream or sugar) and saying very little, unless you take the initiative to start a conversation. Then it soon becomes obvious that he is a very knowledgeable, articulate, and engaging person. One day I struck up a conversation with him and he proceeded to tell me his story:

"When I was discharged some years ago from Ignatia Hall, I tried to do everything they told me: got an AA sponsor (a great man) and attended meetings at least twice a week. About ten years ago my sponsor died, and I started coming here to Ignatia Hall just about every day to sit and watch all these patients going through hell like I did. This reminder each day keeps me sober."

"By the way, Joe," I asked, "how long ago did you come through Ignatia Hall?"

"Next month it will be thirty-five years without a slip," he said. Then he left to do his five miles of jogging for the day.

Who should be treated, and what kind of treatment works? Inpatient or outpatient? Short-term detox or long-term rehabilitation? And where do AA and other self-help groups fit into the picture? These are all complicated questions.

As noted earlier, between 80 and 85 percent of our patients have crossed the line to physical dependency. They will experience the discomfort and pain of withdrawal tremors, sweating, a racing heart, diarrhea, and feeling just terrible when they go through detox. About 95 percent of these patients will also have some type of medical problem, primarily liver injury. Some 35 percent will have stomach problems (ulcers), lung disease (emphysema), heart irregularities, diabetes (elevated blood sugar), or joint problems such as gout. Some of these may require specialized treatment. With or without medical complications, I reiterate my belief that a patient experiencing withdrawal should be hospitalized.

Until recently, hospitalization during withdrawal was the accepted standard of patient care. But now some are proposing that mild to moderate withdrawal can be just as effectively treated outside the hospital in the interests of saving hospital costs. Some insurance companies, as an extension of this cost-saving attitude, insist they will cover costs only if a patient is admitted for a three-day detox treatment and then discharged to enter a less expensive outpatient program. This poses several problems in providing quality health care to our patients. First, the term detox can be very misleading. Some think it means a kind of end point: "If you are detoxed then everything is now OK." Technically, it means the blood alcohol level drops to zero and the tremors, sweating, rapid pulse, and other signs of withdrawal subside. After observing numerous patients go through withdrawal, several things strike me as important: 1) Each patient reacts differently during withdrawal, and 2) subtle but real signs and symptoms persist not only for days, but sometimes weeks which is referred to as a clinical state of protracted withdrawal. Many patients comment on how long it takes to clear their minds.

There is no magical three-day detox, just as the standard twenty-eight-day program is an arbitrary number based more on insurance regulations than on treatment. While some companies will cover only a three-day detox treatment, others will pay benefits only for a full twenty-eight-day program. This puts the treatment centers and sometimes the patient in the middle of a complicated tug-of-war between the insurance companies, focusing on costs and their bottom lines, while health care providers are concerned with finding what's best for their patients.

The upsurge in patients who are admitted with cross-addiction or polydrug abuse has further complicated the length of stay needed for acute cases of withdrawal. The combination of alcohol and cocaine has been the most common cross-addiction, but problems with alcohol and tranquilizers, barbiturates, and various kinds of narcotics remain significant. Remember the case of the former nurse on tranquilizers? She appeared to go into withdrawal from the tranquilizers at the end of a week after apparently completing her withdrawal period from alcohol. As I explained earlier, unlike alcohol, the detox period for most tranquilizers does not become apparent until three to four days after the last dose and then lasts another seven to ten days. Alcohol withdrawal usually starts three to six hours after the last drink and usually lasts from three to six days. Obviously, the three-day detox policy is not going to work safely and effectively for a patient going through tranquilizer or other drug withdrawal in addition to alcohol.

In spite of the comments I've been hearing lately that the pure alcoholic is becoming an endangered species, less than 40 percent of the patients admitted to Ignatia Hall are clinically found to be cross-addicted. This is at a time when treatment centers across the country are reporting an epidemic increase in polydrug patients. During the past year we have also seen an increase in the number of cross-addicted patients, but over 80 percent of our patients insist that alcohol is their chemical of choice. Some of this may be explained by Ignatia Hall's unique fifty-year history as a center specializing in the treatment of alcoholics. However, the conservative social patterns of this Midwestern community probably play a role. I frequently hear comments like "By God, I may be an alcoholic, but I'm no drug addict."

Some have proposed a new medical model of chemical dependency as a disease of addiction, which not only groups the alcoholics with cocaine, heroin, and tranquilizer addicts, but extends the circle to include those with eating disorders, gambling problems, and even cigarette smoking. As a result, we are seeing dramatic changes in treatment philosophies as well as techniques and procedures. Although our staff has enthusiastically embraced this new model of addiction, there is a lesson to be learned from the experience available in treating the disease of cancer. There are many forms and shapes of cancer, and specialized understanding and treatment of the widely different forms is essential for successful outcomes. For cultural, legal, and medical reasons, I feel the same is true for alcoholism treatment. Even though it is part of the expanding list of addictive disorders, I feel alcoholism continues to deserve specialized care and treatment.

To illustrate some of the grey areas of deciding who to treat and how to treat them, let me tell you about three cases after I make one more point. All patients entering our center do so voluntarily, with over 90 percent coming on their own. All through medical school and residency training, physicians have been taught to listen to their patients because they will tell you what is wrong with them. Following this time-honored maxim, it follows that any patient presenting him or herself for admission for a drinking or drug problem should have this self-diagnosis honored and be admitted. Only after admission, however, does the degree and the severity of the problem begin to unfold. To date in our center, there have been no misdiagnoses—when one says he has a drug and alcohol problem on admission, the patient is always right. However, the degree of severity of the problem is the variable which then dictates the kind of treatment.

Case I.   Tim was in his twenties with a history of alcohol and drug abuse dating back to his teens. His wife's union insurance coverage would only pay for a three-day detox. However, based on his history and medical assessment, it was soon clear that Tim was not ready for discharge after three days. Yet because of pressure from the insurance company, coupled with his personal financial situation, we reluctantly discharged him at his request. Four hours later his wife was on the phone with us desperately pleading to readmit him, because as soon as he returned home he had started drinking and taking her "nerve pills." She said, "I'll pay for this somehow, but my husband needs help." Shortly afterwards Tim was readmitted, and his insurance company informed us that they would not cover his hospital stay. Tim stayed a total of twenty-three days in our center. During that time, he apparently went through withdrawal from alcohol, several tranquilizers (Xanax and Valium), and opiates (Demerol and Codeine), and suffered from chronic liver disease. About the fifteenth day of his stay, when his shaking and restlessness had finally started to disappear, Tim revealed for the first time the presence of a headache "that feels like my head is going to blow out the top." Further questioning revealed that these headaches had been bothering him for years. After consulting with a neurologist and using instruments that permitted taking pictures of Tim's brain, our doctors found a small fluid-filled sac in a certain area of his brain which was causing a form of epilepsy. They were able to treat Tim with medicine instead of surgery. He continued to improve and entered a long-term treatment program after discharge. At the present writing, he is doing very well. By the way, the insurance company had second thoughts and paid for the hospital stay.

Case II. Rick was a twenty-nine-year-old car salesman who presented himself for admission to our center. At the time he was admitted, his blood alcohol level was zero and, by his own history, he had not had a drink in about a week. Shortly after admission, his insurance company called, stating that because of these two facts—a zero blood alcohol level and a history of no drinking for one week—his hospital stay would not be covered. The company asked that he be seen in a less expensive outpatient treatment center. It bothered me that this decision was made without knowing the complete history of this patient, and without ever seeing him face to face. In this case I challenged their decision, and I told the company gate keepers, as they were being called, that this man was in need of a structured inpatient treatment program because:

1. This was his first treatment.
2. He was abusing both alcohol and marijuana.
3. He had had five DWIs in the past seven years, the last one a week prior to admission.
4. About one month earlier he had been ordered by the courts to attend a six-day DWI school.
5. His employer had informed him that unless he sought treatment, his job was in jeopardy.

The insurance company physician relented and agreed to cover the patient for six days of an eight-day program. Upon discharge seven days later, the staff felt that the wisdom of our decision was justified when Rick stated:

"You know, when I went through the outpatient program about a month ago I did the same thing during those boring classes as I did in high school; I slept. My mind wasn't on the problems I got into because of alcohol and drugs. I was always thinking about whether I would have enough time after class was over to swing by the bank, or whether I'd have to shovel snow off the driveway, and so on. When I came in here I didn't know what to expect. Actually, this was a form of shock treatment. First the nurse is asking me about my health. Then the doctor comes in and does a complete physical examination. The laboratory people come in and draw blood from my veins and others are taking me down to be X-rayed. I tell you, Doc, I really stopped to take notice and decided right then and there I had better pay attention to what was going on. This really must be serious."

Rick did indeed take the program seriously and was active in all phases of the treatment program during his stay, especially in group sessions where he shared many of the thoughts and feelings that had been bothering him for years. As he was leaving with his recently acquired AA sponsor on the morning of his discharge, he assured us that he would visit and keep us posted on how his program was going. His parting comment was "I really needed this; thank you all."

Case III. Harry's wife was a member of the hospital staff. She made an appointment to see me one day and when I sat down in my office, I didn't have the slightest idea what she wanted. Suddenly she blurted out, "My husband has a drinking problem and I don't know what to do!" If I have learned anything in the past ten years, it is that drinking problems are very prevalent, and not to be surprised at who might have them. Yet I must admit I was surprised at the unexpected disclosure. After hearing some background, I agreed to see her husband *if* he were willing. However, I also insisted that I would want several laboratory tests done before I saw him, namely the mean corpuscular volume test and some liver function tests. I had two reasons for wanting these tests: 1) to determine if any physical damage was taking place in his body as a result of drinking, and 2) to create a sense of seriousness and importance about the situation for all parties concerned, to get everyone's attention. Fortunately, in Harry's case, there was no evidence of any organ damage. Next I suggested that Harry and I meet one-on-one. It seems a rather simple and straightforward request, but I find it important to learn whether the individual will actually keep the appointment or make excuse after excuse about why he or she can't make it. Only two meetings were cancelled before Harry and I met in my office.

I began with my usual series of questions, from "Have you ever been treated for alcoholism?" to "What do you drink and how much?" Having established the apparent severity of Harry's drinking problem in my mind, I proceeded during the next hour and a half to do all of the talking—essentially about everything you have been reading in this book. Through his facial expressions and body language, Harry indicated when I was hitting sensitive spots with slight nods of agreement every now and then as if to say,

"Yes, that's me." In closing I presented him with several
options: 1) meeting with me again, 2) attending AA meetings, or 3) referring him to a counselor. I did not feel he
needed to enter an inpatient treatment program at that
time. He said he wanted to discuss it with his wife before he
decided anything. We said goodnight. "Call me if I can assist
you in any way," I said.

Although I had chance meetings with Harry's wife, we
didn't go beyond the occasional "good morning, how're you
doing" for many months. Then, during a chance meeting in
the medical library, she burst out: "I've been meaning to
thank you for all your help. Harry is doing great. He's
attending AA meetings regularly and hasn't had a drink in
six months. Our life together is great!"

What does all this mean? To me it means that each patient
with a drinking problem needs to be treated on an individualized basis, just as we deal with any patient in attempting to
diagnose the problem and decide on a treatment plan. It also
points out vividly how far we are from having all the answers
to the questions "Who should be treated, and how?" Certainly, in some cases the answers are relatively easy, but there
are many grey areas where the answers become very difficult.
It also emphasizes for me the need for more physicians to be
better informed about the disease of alcoholism and become
more astute in recognizing the signs and symptoms in order
to prescribe the appropriate treatment.

The recent efforts by the American Society of Addiction
Medicine (ASAM) to establish standards for physicians who
care for patients with alcohol and drug problems should be
applauded. I feel this organization's published review course

syllabus should be studied by all practicing physicians. When I suggest to some of my colleagues that they attend some of our treatment activities or attend an AA meeting for their own edification (since as medical students or residents they were never taught anything about alcoholism), they often say indignantly, "I've been treating alcoholics for over twenty years!" Based on the ASAM material and all that I've learned these past ten years from my patients, I'd like to say: "No, you have been treating the physical complications of the disease. The treatment of the disease of alcoholism is a lifelong, ongoing educational and persuasive effort, with the patient focusing on the bottom line: Don't drink alcohol!"

ELEVEN

Relapse

One of the clinical features of any progressive chronic disease is relapse. In alcoholism we sometimes call it a slip or a fall off the wagon or just simply say he started drinking again. We usually reserve the term relapse for someone who has made a concerted effort to deal with a drinking problem by working on his or her sobriety and then slipped. Many of those who have relapsed will seek readmission to an alcoholism treatment program. To readmit or not admit has become a hotly debated issue for many reasons.

In the beginning of the alcoholic ward at St. Thomas Medical Center in 1939, it was Sister Ignatia's strict policy that one was allowed only *one admission* to the ward *in a lifetime*. I suspect the reasoning behind this policy was a form of psychological warfare in dealing with the disease— do this again and you will be punished. Remember, at the time St. Thomas was the only hospital in the area, or indeed perhaps in the nation, to admit alcoholics for regular medical treatment. Sister Ignatia's policy was enforced until the

1950s when new guidelines were established allowing a person a second chance if there was at least a six-month interval since the first admission. This span between admissions was later reduced to ninety days. Today each patient seeking admission following a relapse is evaluated individually. The number of previous admissions and the time between admissions is only part of the basis for deciding who will be readmitted to the center for treatment. But why should the issue of readmission be a consideration at all? Certainly a patient whose diabetes is seriously out of control, or the heart patient who goes into congestive heart failure again, is not denied readmission to a hospital just because he was discharged only several months ago. Why is the alcoholic subjected to this additional barrier to getting treatment? The answer may be the nature of the disease as well as obvious economic considerations.

Alcohol treatment programs can cost from $1,000 to $2,000 to as much as $50,000 to $60,000, depending on the setting, length, and intensity of the treatment. Unfortunately, some patients use alcohol treatment centers in ways similar to those some drug-dependent people use drug treatment centers. As the cost of the addiction increases because their tolerance to the drug increases, getting clean in a drug treatment center brings their tolerance level down, and likewise the cost of the addiction—they need less drug to get the same effects. There are alcoholics who seek help repeatedly to give their bodies a rest so they can go out and start drinking again. As strange as it may sound, these people freely admit, when they voluntarily check themselves into a treatment center, that they are really not ready to stop drinking. Let there be no mistake, these people are drunk, very sick, and need help when they present themselves for admission. However, by repeatedly readmitting them we, the health professionals, become enablers, that is, *someone who is helping to perpetuate the problem rather than resolving the problem*. The rash of new alcohol treatment centers opening across the country in the past few years (this has become a rather lucrative business operation in some instances) has further complicated the situation. The alcoholic who is not ready to quit soon learns how to go treatment-hopping from one facility to another without being challenged by any rules regarding repeat admissions.

Recently, as mentioned, health insurance companies have become tougher, restricting the number of treatments they will pay for and the length of stay for each treatment. The power of the dollar is very real. When a person learns that his insurance will not cover the cost of treatment, especially the cost of extended care, he will usually refuse to enter the program: "Doc, I know I need the help, but I just can't afford it." Unfortunately, there is no guarantee that the person will stop drinking. In fact, the inability to get help may just worsen the problem. Not enough time has elapsed to determine whether this no-pay policy is ultimately in the best interest of the patient. I worry, however, that insurance companies denying payment for professional treatment programs, especially for those patients who have relapsed and are seeking readmission, may result in more serious medical complications down the road. For instance, much recent research is showing that alcohol (ethanol) and the other components of alcoholic beverages, sometimes referred to as congeners, can be directly linked to increased incidences of strokes, cardiac deaths, peptic ulcers and their complications, and a definite increase in the incidence of cancer of the mouth, larynx, and esophagus.

In the long run, I fear a no-pay policy may well be more costly in terms of longer hospital stays and more expensive treatment. Only time will tell.

We have used an individualized approach at Ignatia Hall rather than a herd approach. Instead of the usual practice followed in many alcohol treatment centers of admitting all patients for a preset number of days, whether the patient is a first admission or a repeat admission, we review the patient's history and discuss the presence or absence of medical complications. We consider their attitude, level of interest and motivation (readiness to stop drinking), and, above all, the potential danger a person is to himself or herself. We follow each patient closely after they have been admitted and decide when they should go home based on their progress rather than on a preset number of days. This is followed by an individualized aftercare program, including attending AA meetings after discharge.

Margaret had a lot to do with changing our one-and-only-one admission policy at Ignatia Hall and in dropping our rigid time-between-admissions policy. Margaret had been an executive secretary for a large corporation before her drinking became a problem. Then she began to slide rapidly down until she hit bottom, losing everything, including her job, family, and health. I first met her when she was approaching her fifteenth year of sobriety and had worked her way back up the professional ladder, as well as restoring much of her personal life and health. One day she told me: "I went through about eleven relapses before I was ready to work my program for sobriety. And if I hadn't lied and cheated, and pulled strings to get myself admitted for treatment, I probably never would have made it!" Hearing Margaret's experience was a key factor to tip the scale on our time-honored policy of not readmitting patients who had relapsed or imposing time limits between admissions. Unless the staff evaluation indicates the system is being abused, a relapsed former patient is admitted freely. We concluded that if it took more than one admission for someone like Margaret, who has probably done more for alcoholic women as an AA sponsor during her fifteen years of sobriety than most of us could hope for, then multiple readmissions would no longer be a no-no in our center.

Fred holds the record for readmissions to Ignatia Hall, which number fifteen at last count over a nine-year period. But, for whatever reason, as well as reaching his sixty-ninth birthday, he was ready at last. Fred is now in his fourth year of sobriety, and, medically speaking, is in very good health. Perhaps more important, he is very active in a senior citizens' group dealing with the increasing problem of alcoholism among the elderly. One may say he is probably an exception. Maybe so, but I suspect many of the others who had multiple relapses and did not seek or get treatment for whatever reason in all likelihood drank themselves to death.

You may be wondering by now why the answers to two very important questions have not been discussed: "What causes a relapse?" and "How can you prevent a relapse?" There have been many books on the subject, but my answer to these two questions is very simple: "One, I don't know, and two, don't take the first drink, because you are only one drink away from a drunk."

Our studies demonstrate that those patients who have worked out a plan with their counselor and have followed up with their aftercare counseling and AA meetings on a regular basis after discharge have the best chance of not relapsing. We offer discharge patients one practical piece of AA advice, in addition to the Twelve-Step AA program and one-day-at-a-time philosophy. It is called HALT so it will be easy to remember:

H – Don't allow yourself to get too Hungry.

A – Don't allow yourself to get too Angry.

L – Don't allow yourself to get too Lonely.

T – Don't allow yourself to get too Tired.

If relapse is a characteristic of any chronic disease, we can, in turn, ask the diabetic patient, "Why haven't you followed your diet and taken your insulin regularly?" We could ask the patient with emphysema, "Why did you start smoking again?" We could ask the patient with hypertension, "Why did you go off your low-salt diet?" We could ask the overweight person, "Why did you go off your diet?" Why do people continue to smoke cigarettes when each pack they open has a warning label telling them that what they are doing will hurt them? And, of course, we ask the alcoholic, "Why did you start drinking again?" By far, the most common answer we hear is, "I stopped going to AA meetings and took the first drink."

For now we just have to accept relapses as part of all chronic diseases. Therefore, rather than using the restricted admission policies of treatment centers and insurance companies as a threat, or a big stick, we must acknowledge that all of the patients who have crossed the line to physical dependency are vulnerable to relapse as long as they are alive.

Lately, I have learned of more and more physicians who are telling their diabetic patients, "If you don't control your diet and take your insulin at the proper times, then I would prefer you go to another physician for care" or physicians telling patients who smoke, "If you don't stop smoking, there is no way I can help you with your lung problems and it would be best for you to see another physician." Although one could argue that this is sometimes an effective strategy called tough love, we must be on guard that this type of behavior does not reflect a form of anger, frustration, and even disgust because the patient didn't follow "*my* instructions." My own reaction when one of our former patients is readmitted is to try to reassure them that we are sorry they relapsed and that we understand their embarrassment and shame. However, we try to pick up where we left off and start them once again on the way to recovery.

I believe this approach is beginning to reap some positive benefits, because we are seeing an increasing number of our former patients requesting readmission within a few days of relapse: "Just as you said, Doc, after the first few drinks things started to go downhill real fast. That's why I came back in before I got into real trouble." The result is that they are being readmitted in better physical and emotional shape than if they came in after several months of drinking. This in turn means a shorter hospital stay and a smaller bill. This is progress, slow, but nevertheless progress.

What else can a person learn after being readmitted for the same problem? After all, they have already had the course.

Repetition is a major part, if not the essence, of learning. Just because someone has taken a math course doesn't mean that person knows mathematics. But after acquiring the basic language and techniques, and then trying to apply them on a daily basis while learning more along the way, one comes to know and understand mathematics in a more meaningful way. The same is true for alcoholism. I learn new things every day with each new patient I meet. Alcoholism is something that must be worked on every day for months, years, and even decades. Not everything can be learned during a three-day detox treatment, or an eight-day acute care program, or a twenty-eight-day extended care program. Besides, the changes in brain chemistry from chronic exposure to alcohol can impair memory retention and learning ability for varying periods of time. Many patients who enter our twenty-one-day intermediate care program after spending eight days in our acute care program comment, "I really don't remember very much about what happened during those first eight days, except for a few incidents here and there." No, the treatment program must become a lifetime program, taking it one day at a time. Let's face it, some people are slow learners and some are fast learners. But it is one thing to stay sober in a hospital, another to stay sober at home or out in the world. Unfortunately, some of our patients feel that after they've heard it once, they know it all. "I read the *Big Book (Alcoholics Anonymous,* published by AA) from cover to cover. I'm ready to go home." How foolish! These are the ones who will often be the first to relapse.

Again, let me emphasize that alcoholism is an incurable disease and each person has to learn to live with it for the rest of his or her life. Some will have a harder time than others in accomplishing that goal, but those who stumble and fall along the way deserve our concern, compassion, and patience to get them back on the road to recovery.

TWELVE

A Summing Up

I end each of my talks with a story about Mike. It seems only right that I end this book talking about Mike. Out of misinformation, lack of information, or ignorance, if you will, we build up generalizations and stereotypes of different kinds of people. Because of my own prejudices, the first day I came to Ignatia Hall I expected to see a bunch of grubby-looking old men who had just been picked up out of the gutter. Instead, I saw men and women, young and old, who could have been my father, mother, brother, sister, next-door-neighbor, friend, or fellow worker. I soon learned that the so-called skid row bum or wino makes up less than 3 percent of all alcoholics. My personal shell of prejudice toward the alcoholic had started to crack after those first encounters. It completely disintegrated and crumbled a few years later after meeting Mike.

My office was in the part of the hospital called administration row. The offices of the president, vice-president and chairman of the board of trustees, and other officers of the hospital were all along that hall. One afternoon, while working at my desk, I heard some loud talking in the hallway but paid little attention until I heard a large bellowing voice shout, "Get your f_____g hands off me!" This was so unexpected in the quiet of the hospital that I was sure the bricks would come tumbling down. When that didn't happen, I decided to see what was going on. I stuck my head outside my office door to see two men struggling with each other, one of whom was obviously drunk. By this time everyone else began to peer out to see what was going on. It didn't take anyone long to grasp the nature of the situation. A rowdy, boisterous drunk was making a scene in the hallway. Then all eyes began to look toward me with the obvious message: "Well, you're the expert, do something about this." Remembering what a professor in medical school had told the class one day, "Wear your white coat and make sure they see your stethoscope and no one will hurt you," I ducked back into my office, put on my coat of armor, and went back out into the hallway. Before I could say anything, the man who turned out to be Mike looked at me and bellowed, "Who the f_____ are you?" The other man, who turned out to be his son-in-law, could only say over and over again, "Help me get him to Ignatia Hall."

I introduced myself and finally calmed both men down. I agreed to accompany them upstairs to Ignatia Hall. As we were riding up in the elevator, the situation approached the level of tension where it felt like someone had to say something. I had tried earlier to engage Mike in conversation, and all his comments were f_____ this or f_____ that, in a bellowing voice that rang down the hallways. Many hospital visitors' heads turned upon hearing these remarks and the expression on their faces reflected a feeling of distaste or disgust towards Mike. So we had just walked in silence until the elevator ride. Then I noticed that Mike had a tattoo on his arm—U.S.M.C., with a Marine Corps insignia. I thought this could be a starting point for conversation, so I said, "Mike, I see you were in the Marines."

"What the f_____ is it to you?"

"Well, I was in the Navy." That was a mistake. In the thirty-plus years since I had left the Navy, I had forgotten about the intense rivalry between the Navy and the Marines. Before I could retrieve this warning from my memory bank, here came a powerful right swing at my head, as he bellowed, "Why, you no good f_____g swab jockey!" Fortunately, I ducked, and the stainless steel wall of the elevator took the force of the blow. Just then the elevator door opened and now I, too, was shouting, "Help me get this man into Ignatia Hall!" The experienced nursing staff quickly calmed Mike down, and he was admitted to the center without further incident.

Four or five days later, I told this story in much the same words to our patients, including Mike, in the weekly afternoon talk. Everyone started looking around, wondering who in the world I was talking about, because they were convinced there was no one in the group who would exhibit such behavior. You see, in those four or five days, as Mike sobered up, he proved to be one of the nicest, kindest, most caring human beings I have ever met. He was helping all the patients and the staff and had gained the love and respect of everyone. The lesson to be learned was that during my first contact with Mike he was wearing the mask of alcohol. The mask was disguising his true self and, as the effect of the alcohol wore off, I came to learn who Mike, the person, really was—a wonderful human being

No one likes an intoxicated person, or more bluntly, a drunk. Their behavior is so unpredictable. They may be funny, sad, angry, hostile, belligerent, loud, boisterous, obscene, annoying, even dangerous to those around them as well as to themselves. To compound the problem, there is almost a sense of disgust on the part of uninvolved third-party observers that an individual would let himself get into that condition. Unfortunately, when you mention the word alcoholic, the image that is most often conjured up in the public's mind is just what we have described, a sorry excuse for a man or woman.

I consider myself fortunate because I have seen the loud, obscene, belligerent, angry, annoying, and sad excuse for a man or woman come to our center. Then, as they shed the mask and disguise of alcohol over the next several days, there emerges in most instances a very wonderful human being whom I feel privileged to know. Oh yes, there are times, thankfully relatively few, when the mask is removed and there emerges a personality that is more than we had bargained for, but that is very rare.

The point of all this is that anyone who drinks alcohol can become drunk and act in an annoying and disgusting manner, and, of course, this includes an alcoholic. But the alcoholic, during recovery, takes off that mask. It continues to inspire me to visit an AA meeting and hear the person giving the lead get up and say, "Hi, my name is _____, I'm an alcoholic" with almost a sense of pride and conviction.

The greatest challenge for all of us is to help that person, and all other alcoholics, to keep from ever putting on that familiar mask again after it has been stripped off. Or, better still, to help them not to put it on in the first place.

THIRTEEN

Some Thoughts About the Future

AA's successful teaching to take one day at a time was never intended to exclude looking to the future. On the contrary, it suggests that you take one step after another, making sure you are on solid footing rather than trying to solve all of your problems overnight. So it is with the disease of alcoholism. The likelihood of a miracle cure tomorrow is very remote, but we must keep moving forward toward the future to better understand this very complex disease. There is no quick fix.

As we look to the future, I think five areas appear especially promising and may deserve greater attention: 1) first and foremost, the attitudes of the public surrounding this problem, 2) how genetic studies can assist us in predicting and preventing the disease, 3) how changes in the chemistry of certain parts of the brain can influence our everyday behavior, 4) the role of what we eat on brain chemistry and our everyday behavior, and 5) the role of biofeedback techniques as a means to bring about lasting behavioral modifications.

Changing Attitudes

Let's start with the attitudes. One of my biggest problems when I first became director of Ignatia Hall was my reaction to patients referring to one another as a drunk in the regular course of conversation, or to having an AA visitor refer to one of our patients as an alcoholic without batting an eyelash. To me, at that time, to call someone a drunk or an alcoholic was one of the lowest forms of insult because of the stereotyped image I had of people who had an alcohol problem. I still feel a little uncomfortable whenever someone refers to anyone as a drunk, even though I have come to realize that this is okay for someone in a group of alcoholics. I have no problem today talking about an alcoholic patient just as one speaks of a diabetic or a cardiac patient. Please do not misunderstand; I still get annoyed and upset today as I did in the early days when I see someone staggering down the street, shouting obscenities, talking gibberish with slurred speech, or wanting to fight everyone within reach. However, today I try to imagine how this same person will be acting and appearing several days down the road when he is sober. A slobbering, staggering, disabled human being under the influence of alcohol can present a disgusting sight, to say the least. And if that person has just been responsible for killing or injuring another human being in a car accident, I can understand how the hate and anger of a lynch mob mentality can develop.

The quick fix for the problems of drinking behavior and drunken drivers has always been to pass stricter laws and have the courts hand out more severe punishments. The realistic solution, which takes more time, is to have much more public education about the consequences and effects of drinking alcohol. But since the majority of people who drink alcohol have gained the impression that they can handle it, we find that a prevalent attitude toward the alcoholic or anyone who gets in trouble with the bottle is "I can handle it, why can't you?" This sense of superiority provides a false security, because there is a very thin and fragile dividing line between able to handle it and unable to handle it.

This judgemental attitude toward the alcoholic has to be changed to "Yes, I can understand why you can't handle it, let us help you." We can express this attitude in many capacities: as a health professional ("Let me be more caring and understanding."); as a family member or friend ("Let me be more supportive."); as a public official ("Let me facilitate the flow of resources for treatment and research."); and as a private citizen ("Let me contribute time or money to further our understanding of this disease.").

I hasten to add that this caring attitude need not be carried to the extreme of excusing *any* person from receiving some form of punishment for a criminal offense that was committed while under the influence of alcohol. For instance, a twenty-two-year-old college senior under the influence of alcohol failed to negotiate a curve while driving, lost control of the car, and in the aftermath his eighteen-year-old friend was killed. He should not be totally absolved of responsibility for the tragic event. He must be held accountable for his actions. Agreed, he is not a hardened criminal. As a matter of fact, a psychosocial history as well as a complete medical history would permit the diagnosis of a social-impulsive type of drinker. The accident I described occurred while the student was driving back to the dormitory after a post-victory soccer team party, which traditionally included a keg of beer. But the reality is there for all to see. A life was taken because he was drunk. In this case, the jury and judge took many factors into consideration in handing down a guilty verdict and a prison sentence. But there was punishment.

The logical solution is, of course, to eliminate the causative factor, the alcohol. History has taught us that this approach has failed before and there is no reason to believe it wouldn't fail again. As I was taught in my premedical college studies, man has a free will and he will act as he sees fit. The growth and prosperity of the advertising industry has been built on these foundations. The result is two kind-looking, elderly gentlemen on television (they remind me of my grandfather) telling us, in effect, that it is okay to drink a certain brand of wine cooler, or various sports heroes telling us what's so great about a certain kind of beer. Some would have us try another quick-fix approach and ban all alcoholic-beverage advertising, or at least control it. Frankly, this approach would probably be as unsuccessful as the warning label on cigarette packages. It could also lead to putting labels on milk cartons warning that the fat content of milk can cause atherosclerosis or to removing all salt from foods to prevent hypertension and strokes. The answer really rests with the individual, who must assume more responsibility for his or her own health.

I learned something else in college and that is that man is a rational being, capable of taking in information and making rational decisions that take into account the consequences of those decisions. In other words, we can teach people about alcohol and its damaging effects on their bodies and their lives in general and let them, through their own free will, decide not to drink alcohol. I know this approach works, because in many, many instances this is the whole basis for the treatment of alcoholism. Our only tools are education and persuasion, whether in the home, the classroom, billboards, television, or radio—a form of advertising if you will, but in this case we are selling health. Unfortunately, health is not viewed as a very exciting product by many people, until they wish they had it.

I emphasize again and again, especially with younger people, that alcohol is a pharmacologic agent or drug that, depending on the amount consumed or the "dose," can cause impairment or defects in our vision, our hearing, our depth perception, our reaction speed, our performance on accuracy tasks, our information processing, our attention span, our behavioral compensation and control, our scanning behavior, our memory, our mood and emotions. These effects can occur in anyone who drinks alcoholic beverages, whether they have developed the disease of alcoholism or not.

This educational process will take time, but even if it is slow in coming, the alcoholic must not sit around and wait, but must assume personal responsibility for himself or herself. No one else can do it for you. First you must take care of yourself before you can help in taking care of others.

Genetic Studies

Where is research taking us? In the past several years I have been hearing more patients and recovering alcoholics refer to my disease or your disease. More are asking questions like, "Doc, is my disease inherited?" or "Will my children become alcoholics?" or "What should I tell my kids?" Still others have introduced biochemical terms into their vocabularies, like THIQs or endorphins or neurotransmitters. Others have been describing to me a sure-fire diet that will cut down on the craving for alcohol. These comments and questions focus on several major areas of research taking place in clinics and laboratories around the world. Researchers are seeking specific answers to questions like: 1) is alcoholism inherited?, 2) is abnormal behavior caused by abnormal brain chemistry?, 3) can what you eat change your behavior because it can change the chemistry in your brain?, and 4) does the technique of biofeedback have a place in the treatment of alcoholism? The accumulating evidence leaves little doubt that the answer to each of these questions is a resounding "*Yes! But* we still have much to learn."

Let's look at each of these areas a little more closely. Although a detailed review of these studies would be way beyond the scope of this book, I'd like to give you a taste of what's going on. We can all take some encouragement and hope from the fact that something is being done. But at this stage much of the research is still in the realm of speculation and theories. Too much enthusiasm can raise false hope and subsequent disappointment for those suffering with the problem today. So I want to temper optimism with a touch of realism and caution.

As mentioned earlier, approximately 50 percent of the patients admitted to our treatment center had or have alcoholic fathers. It was also noted that over thirty families have had three generations of men treated in the center over a span of fifty years. The idea that alcoholism is an inherited disease is far from new. For instance, over 2,300 years ago

Plutarch wrote about drunkenness running in families. However, only recently has the distinction between the role of genetic factors and the role of environmental factors been addressed. Just because an alcoholic patient had a father who was an alcoholic is not positive proof that the disease was inherited. One could argue that there was an environmental effect. The son saw the father drink and thought it was appropriate to drink himself—like father, like son.

The adoption studies that were carried out in two Scandinavian countries where public records were carefully compiled for many years offered an opportunity for the first time to separate the role of genetic and environmental factors. More importantly, these studies provided convincing (though not conclusive) evidence that the tendency to develop alcoholism is inherited.

In similar studies conducted in other parts of the world, the results have been generally similar. I should add that as more data are collected, it has become increasingly evident that there is much interaction between genetic and environmental factors—that is, instead of acting independently, they act together. For instance, you could inherit the predisposition to develop the disease of alcoholism from either or both of your parents, yet if you never drank alcohol in your life, you would never develop the signs and symptoms of alcoholism.

Let's look a little more closely at the meaning of genetic predisposition. It is worth mentioning at this point our analogy of two people marooned on a deserted island. One has a genetic predisposition to cancer which is inherited from either or both parents, while the other does not. There are no cancer-causing agents (excluding sunlight, of course) polluting the island. There are no cancer-causing viruses or chemical carcinogens, no artificial radiation, and they are both nonsmokers. In this relatively cancer-free environment, neither individual should develop cancer. On the other hand, if the same two people were living in a polluted environment, then the one with the genetic predisposition would develop cancer and the other would not, in spite of being exposed to the same carcinogenic agents. This is the main reason why the argument about cigarette smoking and lung cancer goes on and on. To the man in the street who is told to stop smoking because it will cause lung cancer, his answer could be, "My father lived until he was 90 years old and smoked cigarettes from the time he was ten years old!" Conclusion: his father was not genetically predisposed to develop lung cancer.

Another example of genetic predisposition can be seen in the experience in Vietnam, where reports indicated that thousands of U.S. servicemen from all walks of life used heroin while stationed there. It was readily available, and many servicemen became physically dependent. However, upon returning to the States, only a relatively small percentage became dependent on heroin again. The difference in percentages suggests that there was a genetic predisposition to develop heroin dependency in only a small percentage of returning servicemen.

Genetic predisposition is a rather general concept, and scientists have been attempting to define what this means in more specific terms, namely in terms of specific molecules within the cells of the body. The genes, which are molecules of a chemical called DNA, are transferred from your mother and father to all the cells in your body following fertilization and further growth and development. Recently, in the course of searching for the "alcoholism gene," scientists have reported the presence of a specific gene (D_2, dopamine receptor gene) that may increase one's susceptibility to alcoholism. However, the finding has been challenged by other studies, and still others have questioned how a single gene could be so strongly associated with a common disorder that is known to be very complex and to affect so many different types of people. Each person's genes control their cells' machinery to make new molecules, including the enzymes that are responsible for speeding the build-up or breaking down of different molecules within the body (metabolism). Alcohol, when absorbed into the body, is broken down by one of these enzymes located in the liver. This chemical reaction turns alcohol into acetaldehyde and eventually into carbon dioxide, water, and heat. The presence of this enzyme, and how active it is in the cell, is determined by the genes that characterize the individual. We can measure this difference indirectly by measuring how rapidly the acetaldehyde in the blood increases after one drinks some alcohol. It has been suggested that alcoholics have a higher level of acetaldehyde after drinking than nonalcoholics.

This type of study also suggests that it might be possible to test brothers and sisters of alcoholics, and by the rate at which the acetaldehyde forms after a drink of alcohol determine which ones are genetically predisposed to develop the disease and which ones are not. It may eventually be possible to predict at the time of birth who will and will not be predisposed to become an alcoholic. And with early education, the development of the disease in later life could be prevented. This is not a science fiction-type of thinking. We already have evidence that leans in this direction.

The case in point is the relatively low incidence of alcoholism in Oriental populations. Approximately 60 percent of Orientals experience a flushing of the face and an increased heart rate as well as sweating within minutes and even seconds of swallowing a drink of an alcoholic beverage. These clinical findings are correlated with a high level of acetaldehyde in the blood, which is due to a genetically-determined level of the alcohol-metabolizing enzyme in Oriental people. It is assumed that with almost immediate flushing, sweating, and palpitations every time you drink alcohol, one decides to avoid it. This is called a type of aversion reaction. Simply stated, if you eat or drink something that makes you sick, you stay away from it. Orientals have a relatively low incidence of alcoholism.

There may be strong environmental factors at work as well. Awhile back I attended a formal dinner with a medical student of Chinese parentage. Wine was being served, and I was curious as to whether this young student was going to drink his wine or not. When it became apparent he was not going to drink it, I began to ask him some questions about his experience with alcohol. He told me that from the time he was three years old his parents and grandparents told him never to touch a drop of alcohol because it would make him sick. "I believed my parents and followed their instructions very conscientiously through high school. Then I went to college and I tried my first glass of wine to be one of the group. You know what?" he said. "My parents were right. I became very ill and I haven't touched a drop of alcohol since that time."

Other exciting research may prove helpful in detecting those individuals in a family or the population in general who have a predisposition to develop the disease. Some studies show that the brain waves of sons of alcoholic fathers are different from the brain waves of subjects who have no family history of alcoholism. Also, changes in the hormone levels of men whose fathers are alcoholics were found to be different from those of men whose fathers were not alcoholics after both groups had several drinks of alcohol.

The point of all this is not only to understand better how the disease works, but to identify, if possible, genetically predisposed alcoholics at early stages and then, through early education and appropriate environmental influence, possibly prevent the disease and its complications from ever developing. At the present time, when any of my patients ask me "What shall I tell my kids?", my reply has been general, since we are not yet in the position to say who is and who is not genetically predisposed to become an alcoholic. "The best solution," I usually say, "is to set them down and try to educate them about the disease." I hope this book will prove helpful.

In an earlier section, we also talked about how laboratory animals can be used to study the role of genetic factors in alcoholism. You may recall that certain strains of mice and rats have been shown to have a preference for alcohol-containing water as opposed to plain water. Even the female golden hamsters that have become popular as household pets appear to have this preference for alcohol. In general, most animals have an aversion to alcohol, except for these uniquely bred strains of rats and mice. There is some question whether the role of genetics is acting on the chemistry of the brain to bring about a preference-seeking behavior for alcohol, or whether this is a genetically determined preference for the taste that acts on the taste buds of the tongue. No matter, these animals provide a powerful tool in investigating the interaction of alcohol with body chemistry, and particularly with the chemistry of the brain.

Biochemistry of the Brain

Genetics, by definition, relates to biochemical reactions throughout the body. Recent advances in understanding the chemistry of the brain have placed the field of neurobiology in the forefront of scientific research today. Based upon recent findings in this discipline, it is becoming increasingly accepted that all behavior has a chemical basis in the brain. Furthermore, it has been shown that the chemicals called neurotransmitters, which move messages from one nerve cell to another across a synapse, or gap, between the end of one nerve cell and the beginning of another, can cause some cells to speed up and others to be slowed down in different parts of the brain. This has provided a fertile field of study for the discipline of behavioral pharmacology: that is, the design and study of different drugs that act on certain parts of the brain to bring about changes in behavior. It is amazing to me that laboratory animals like mice, rats, and monkeys, with needle-thin tubes placed in different parts of the brain, will press a lever repeatedly to give themselves a shot (called self-administration) if the drug is cocaine or morphine, but will not press the lever repeatedly if the drug is aspirin, digitalis, or some of the antidepressants. The compulsion to self-administer cocaine, as mentioned, can be so strong that the animal can actually kill itself. Of great importance is the fact that these animals will self-administer the same drugs that humans self-administer.

It appears that these specific drugs like cocaine and morphine act either directly or indirectly upon a part of the brain called the reward system, or as some refer to it, "the happy center." It has been proposed that there is a chemical signal released in the brain when cocaine or morphine are injected that says "This feels good, do it again" and "again" and "again." There is reason to believe that alcohol or its breakdown product, acetaldehyde, can alter the neurotransmitters of the brain to produce a substance called tetrahydroisoquinolone (THIQ), which can produce the same kind of response in the happy center as that produced by cocaine or morphine. More and more evidence is accumulating to support the idea that the craving for these drugs is related to an altered brain chemistry of this part of the brain, and that this altered brain chemistry is determined most strongly by genetic factors. Theoretically, a nonalcoholic's happy center would be satisfied with a minimal level of stimulation, but an alcoholic's would never be stimulated enough. Like the animal who self-administers cocaine until it overdoses and dies, the alcoholic can self-administer alcohol until death.

The problem becomes even more intriguing when we learn that the body produces its own chemicals that act like morphine. These are called endorphins. More recently, morphine itself has been found in the brains of laboratory animals. These findings have led to the speculation that people who are genetically predisposed to use morphine are so because their happy centers are deficient in the morphine synthesized by the body; thus, they self-medicate with morphine to fill the deficiency. In the process, the individual becomes addicted and physically dependent upon the morphine. It could follow, using this line of reasoning, that the alcoholic's happy center is deficient in some metabolic product of alcohol metabolism, or even deficient in alcohol itself, and so one drinks to make up for the deficiency. The deficiency in the happy center is caused by genetic factors acting through biochemical reactions.

Alcohol and Nutrition

The saying "we are what we eat" became popular in the sixties and seventies, although the idea has probably been around for centuries. At first, perhaps, the obvious effects of the amounts and kinds of food eaten were related to the physical appearance of the body. Then the focus began to narrow to the effects of diet on health and the development of certain diseases, like the link between cholesterol and heart disease, or between salt and hypertension, or excess calories and obesity. Now evidence is adding up to show that what we eat can affect our behavior, like feeling depressed, hyperactive, or even sleepy.

It has been known for some time that the chemical serotonin is one of the many neurotransmitters in our brains that can cause a slow-down of cell activity in certain parts of the brain, which results in the subject's being less anxious and actually becoming sleepy. It is not possible to get this effect by injecting serotonin, or by taking it by mouth, because it cannot get from the circulating blood into the brain cells due to the presence of what is called a blood-brain barrier. On the other hand, when we eat the naturally occurring amino acid L-tryptophane, which is present in many of the foods we consume every day, our body converts the L-tryptophane into serotonin. L-tryptophane can cross the blood-brain barrier, and once it gets into the brain tissue, it can be readily converted to serotonin. Taking this naturally occurring chemical either in one's regular diet or as a supplement to the diet should have a calming effect on the individual. This is exactly what has been shown in a clinical setting. We gave 1,000 to 2,000 milligrams (mgs) of L-tryptophane about thirty minutes before bedtime to our patients with sleeping problems. About 75 percent of the patients showed an improvement in sleep, both subjectively and objectively, as compared to placebos. The tradition of a glass of warm milk at bedtime works because milk contains fairly high concentrations of L-tryptophane. Also, the familiar sleepy feeling after a traditional Thanksgiving Day turkey dinner may be related in part to the high concentrations of L-tryptophane in turkey, especially in the white meat. It has also been shown that diets rich in carbohydrates will cause an increase in the serotonin level of the brain, while a diet high in proteins will cause a decrease in the serotonin level.

Unfortunately, L-tryptophane has recently been removed from the market because it was linked to a serious and sometimes fatal condition called eosinophilia-myalgia. The evidence now points to a contaminant in the preparation rather than the L-tryptophane itself as the causative factor. Hopefully, this naturally-occurring amino acid will again be available for medical use.

Much has been written about the connection between hyperactivity in children and sugar consumption. Reducing sugar intake has been one of the usual treatment strategies. However, researchers have recently raised the question of whether, just like an adult who takes a tranquilizer to calm down, a hyperactive child is eating excessive sugars and sweets to raise the serotonin levels of the brain and actually trying to calm down.

Along the same lines of thinking, we know that the amino acids phenylalanine and tyrosine in our diet are converted to dopamine, norepinephrine, and epinephrine in the body. These neurotransmitters tend to be capable of speeding up nerve cell activity, and it has been proposed that dietary phenylalanine and tyrosine or supplements can alleviate depression. Without going into further detail, the bottom line is that nutrition can affect brain chemistry, which in turn can affect behavior.

Several alcohol treatment centers throughout the world are beginning to use amino acid supplements as well as planned diets to bring about certain behavioral changes in the alcoholic patient. I suspect the number of centers using this dietary approach is on the rise. It's my personal opinion that we are on the threshold of some of the greatest breakthroughs in nutritional research that we have ever seen.

Biofeedback and Behavior Modification

Behavior modification, simply stated, is the attempt to change habits or behaviors, like learning how to cope with stress, or learning how to relax. Since our understanding of brain chemistry and attempts to modify it are still in their infancy, we keep looking for a shortcut. The alcoholic, the person who is obese, the cigarette smoker, or the gambler are all frustrated: "I know I shouldn't drink, eat, smoke, or gamble, but I just can't help it." It is possible that behavior modification techniques can bring about changes in brain chemistry, too. Recent work with biofeedback suggests that what we feel can influence our heart rate and our blood pressure, or even prevent epileptic seizures in certain individuals. At one time we thought the heart rate and blood pressure and certain other body functions were under some type of involuntary control, as compared to voluntary control whereby we can willfully walk or use our hands or feet. Now we know that learning how to think about these functions can slow down the heart rate or decrease the blood pressure. Simply stated, we have to continually try to learn how to listen to the messages our body is sending to us and then translate those messages into behavioral changes or modifications. It is tempting to speculate that the successful history of AA could be related in part to a type of biofeedback event: the pattern of regularly attending meetings, the persistent reinforcement not to drink again, the philosophy of taking one day at a time, and acknowledging the existence of a higher power—all keep the problem in the forefront of consciousness. This type of concentrated thinking could bring about changes in body functions resulting in a reduction of craving for alcohol, which could become a permanent behavior pattern. After all, there are people who reach more than thirty years of sobriety using the AA method.

Alcohol research, along with research in the areas of neurobiology, behavioral pharmacology, and nutritional behavior modification, are moving along at an unprecedented rate, making it next to impossible to keep abreast of all the advances taking place. The transfer time from the research laboratory to the clinical setting, with practical use of a new discovery, can take months and years. This can be very frustrating for a person waiting for a cure to a particular disease. The pressure for quick fixes is always there, but the careful and conscientious investigator will make certain of all of the facts before promoting a certain treatment, which, in turn, could prove to bring disappointment and failure. In spite of the tremendously exciting new information in the areas of genetics, neurobiology, behavioral pharmacology, and nutrition, the best scientific advice and assistance that can be given to the alcoholic patient at this time is *Abstinence*, which is the same message and advice that was the starting point for AA in 1935. I guess one could say that nothing much has changed, but, in fact, it really has: we are now working from a stronger base of understanding rather than from myths and ignorance.

I have learned most of what I know about alcoholism from taking care of my patients and from the many members of AA who visit our center on a regular basis, always providing some words of wisdom. In fact, at the time of first writing this section, I was greeted by one of our regular AA visitors as I was getting off the elevator. There was nothing special about his "Good morning, Doc," this particular morning, because he has greeted me this way practically every morning for the past five years. But a little later, as I was hurrying to the elevator to go to a meeting, he stopped me and said quietly, but with obvious pride and delight, "Today makes it thirty-one years!" Obviously, he wasn't talking about his birthday, since he is in his sixties. No, I knew what he was talking about—he had been sober for thirty-one years! Frankly, I was so thrilled I wanted to hug him, but before I could he said in a serious tone, "The only way I was able to do it was by taking one day at a time, by accepting that I was powerless over alcohol and accepting a higher power."

I have written little about the spiritual aspect of treating alcoholism in this book because 1) I do not feel qualified to talk about this topic, and 2) this is a very personal relationship that different people view in different ways. Its omission from this discussion in no way reflects a lack of importance, which brings to mind my encounter with Richard.

Richard is a successful and prominent businessman in his community who was rapidly losing everything—family, business, home, and, above all, his health—when he presented himself at our center for treatment. Following a family intervention, he had agreed most begrudgingly to seek help and, to say the least, he was a very angry person. Before I even had a chance to introduce myself as I prepared to carry out his medical examination, he blurted out, "Doc, I don't want any of this goddam praying stuff, I'm an atheist!"

Although one becomes accustomed to seeing and hearing things in medicine that many could consider bizarre or at least inappropriate behavior, I must say I was taken aback for a moment. After dealing with over 6,000 alcoholic patients, this was the first time one of them was so blunt and determined to ensure that I was aware of his purported lack of religious beliefs. Others may have had similar feelings, but no one had expressed them as Richard did that morning. Then, just eight days later, a rather amazing thing happened. Richard motioned me apart from the other patients and in a most calm and sincere manner said, "Doc, I want to tell you something." Again, I've become used to surprises from my patients, but I must admit I was exceptionally curious in this instance. "Last night," Richard continued, "I did something I haven't done since I was thirteen years old—I got down on my knees and I prayed." The meeting of our eyes and the touch of our hands said everything, and no words were exchanged. Of course, he didn't see the goose flesh all over my body as I heard these words. Richard, as of today, is doing very well. He visits the center almost every morning and participates with the patients in the morning meditation. His smile and positive outlook on life proves to be an inspiration to all.

The saying "one day at a time" is repeated often among recovering alcoholics, but only those who embrace its deep-seated spiritual meaning prove to be the most successful at remaining sober. Even nonalcoholics would do well to embrace this philosophy because it provides an opportunity to arrange the priorities in your life, and, above all, to live each day to the fullest. As I tell my patients when hopelessness is foremost in their minds: "As long as the sun comes up each morning, there is hope. Remember, each sunrise brings a new day!" Scientists are unraveling the complexities and mysteries of the disease of alcoholism, and I believe progress will see this disease being managed and controlled like other chronic diseases such as diabetes, heart disease, and cancer. But as we inch along in this direction, all we have is hope and living one day at a time.

FURTHER READING

Alcoholics Anonymous. *Alcoholics Anonymous: The Story of How Many Thousands of Men and Women Have Recovered From Alcoholism*. New York: Alcoholics Anonymous World Services, Inc., 1976.

Alcoholics Anonymous. *Alcoholics Anonymous Comes of Age: A Brief History of A.A.* New York: Alcoholics Anonymous World Services, Inc., 1957.

Alcoholics Anonymous. *Profile of an A.A. Meeting*. New York: Alcoholics Anonymous World Services, Inc., 1972.

Crow, K.E. and Batt, R.O., eds. *Human Metabolism of Alcohol*, Vols. I, II, and III. Boca Raton, Florida: CRC Press Inc., 1989.

Gitlow, S.E. and Peyser, H., eds. *Alcoholism: A Practical Treatment Guide*. New York: Grune and Stratton, 1980.

Jellinek, E.M. *The Disease Concept of Alcoholism*. New Haven: Hill House, 1960.

Ketchum, K. and Mueller, L.A. *Eating Right to Live Sober: A Comprehensive Guide to Alcoholism and Nutrition*. Seattle, Wa.: Madrona Publishers, 1983.

Sandmaier, M. *The Invisible Alcoholic: Women and Alcohol Abuse in America*. New York: McGraw-Hill, 1981.

Vaillant, G.E. *The Natural History of Alcoholism: Causes, Patterns and Paths to Recovery*. Cambridge, Mass.: Harvard University Press, 1983.

ABOUT THE AUTHOR

Robert Liebelt began his medical career after earning both a Ph.D. and an M.D. with honors from Baylor College of Medicine. He served as chairman and professor of anatomy for eighteen years at Baylor, where he dedicated himself to the classroom: teaching medical students, nursing students, pre- and post-doctoral Biomedical Science trainees and other health care professional students. Dr. Liebelt carried on experimental laboratory studies in the fields of nutrition, obesity, and cancer research. He later became the provost of the Medical College of Georgia. Dr. Liebelt was the charter dean and, later, provost dean of the newly-created Northeastern Ohio Universities College of Medicine in Rootstown, Ohio.

He joined the medical staff of St. Thomas Medical Center (formerly St. Thomas Hospital) in January 1978 where he became a member of the Department of Family Practice and, later, director of medical education. In 1982, he became director of the Ignatia Hall Acute Alcohol Treatment Center.

In 1985, Dr. Liebelt helped found the Robert H. Smith, M.D. Interim Care Center. He is also presently serving as vice president of medical education at the hospital as well as associate dean for clinical science and a professor for the Northeastern Ohio Universities College of Medicine.

Dr. Liebelt continues to teach, to speak publicly, and to devote time to laboratory and clinical research focusing on the genetics of alcoholism. In 1988 he received certification from the American Society for Addiction Medicine. In 1989 he was the honored recipient of the Akron community's Doug Dieken Award for Courage.

Index